day trade
part-time

Wiley Online Trading for a Living

Electronic Day Trading to Win/Bob Baird and Craig McBurney

Day Trade Part-Time/John Cook and Jeanette Szwec

The Strategic Electronic Day Trader/Robert Deel

Day Trade Online/Christopher A. Farrell

Trade Options Online/George A. Fontanills

Electronic Day Trading 101/Sunny J. Harris

Trade Stocks Online/Mark Larson

How I Trade for a Living/Gary Smith

Day Trade Futures Online/Larry Williams

Trade IPOs Online/Matthew D. Zito and Matt Olejarczyk

day trade
part-time

JOHN COOK
JEANETTE SZWEC

John Wiley & Sons, Inc.

New York • Chichester • Weinheim • Brisbane • Singapore • Toronto

Published by John Wiley & Sons, Inc.

Published simultaneously in Canada.

This publication is designed to provide accurate and authoritative information in regard to the subject matter covered. It is sold with the understanding that the publisher is not engaged in rendering legal, accounting, or other professional services. If legal advice or other expert assistance is required, the services of a competent professional person should be sought.

The authors assume no responsibility for actions taken by readers. The authors are not providing investment advice. The authors do not make any claims, promises, or guarantees that any suggestions, systems, trading strategies, or information will result in a profit, loss, or any other desired result. All readers assume all risk, including but not limited to the risk of losses, which could exceed investment capital. (The risk of loss in day trading can be substantial. Only use "risk" capital for day trading.)

Designations used by companies to distinguish their products are often claimed as trademarks. In all instances where John Wiley & Sons, Inc. is aware of a claim, the product names appear in initial capital or all capital letters. Readers, however, should contact the appropriate companies for more complete information regarding trademarks and registration.

Library of Congress Cataloging-in-Publication Data:

Cook, John, 1942–
    Day trade part-time / John Cook and Jeanette Szwec.
      p.   cm.—(Wiley on-line trading for a living)
    ISBN 0-471-39310-X (cloth : alk. paper)
    1. Electronic trading of securities.   2. Day trading (Securities)
 I. Szwec, Jeanette, 1947–   II. Title.   III. Series.
 HG4515.95 .C664   2000
 332.64'0285—dc21   00-036650

Printed in the United States of America

10 9 8 7 6 5 4 3 2 1

To our sons

Zach and Mike,
*may they always
pursue their dreams.*

preface

We are two professional day traders who have made every mistake imaginable on our road to profitability. It does not have to be that way. We have written this book for the potential part-time day trader. Our goal is to let you enter this exciting field in a simpler, less costly manner.

how this book began

We met on-line in the trading room run by The UndergroundTrader called "The Trading Pit." We had both been trading for some time and struck up a conversation about trading techniques one day after hours. We came from a similar background of training—John had gone through Jay Yu's real-time training program, and Jeanette had taken Jay's self-study course. In fact, it was our trust in Jay and his techniques that led us both to join the UndergroundTrader trading room.

Over time, we started to use each other to test theories, to test trading thoughts, to compare strategies, and later to cheer or console one another, depending on the day. We started talking about the psychology of our trading—trying to explain the mistakes we each made and seeking understanding from each other on why we had made some of them. We started talking about our early trading experiences and our frustrations relating to the process of learning how to day trade. We laughed together about our experiences day trading with our on-line discount brokerage accounts and moaned to each other about how our financial resources were eaten up because of our lack of direction on how to start this day trading thing. And we wished we could do something to make this easier for people who were just learning.

At first, we started mentoring others in a trading room, answering questions about software, brokerages, and our use of the futures to help our trading decisions. Then we started documenting our answers, thinking we could teach a course where we shared some of this information. One day we realized that these notes were very comprehensive, that many people could benefit from this information, and that we could help new traders save time and money if we could share our experiences with them. We felt we could help others avoid the frustration of depleted capital and the discouragement that comes from making so many mistakes because they have no good path to follow. We decided to compile the information from these notes into a book to help people who had the desire to trade.

We met in person for the first time after we had completed the first draft of this book. It seems only fitting that our book about day trading using the Internet was written entirely by communicating and sharing over the Internet.

why this book was written

When we started day trading, there was no one place to ask, "Where and how can I learn to day trade?" Like most traders, we found the process of gathering information about trading to be inefficient, expensive, and in some cases, misleading. *Day Trade Part-Time* will help you answer the questions "Should I trade or not?" and "Should I become a part-time day trader?" If you want to trade, we will show you how to get started, and we will give you the information and resources to do so. No fluff; all straight talk!

We are just ordinary people who wanted to day trade. Most authors writing about day trading come from a Wall Street background. They are market makers, brokers, and hedge fund managers—people totally familiar with the inner workings of the market. They are bright, smart, young, but totally unrepresentative of the majority of the potential day trading population. Most people considering day trading were not born on Wall Street. They are the common "Joes and Janes" of the world—independent spirits who want to try something challenging that can give them a new source of income. We come from the same type of background that most potential traders come from. One of us is an entrepreneur; one is a single mother who needed a source of income to support her son in college. We are everyday people who don't have Wall Street contacts or Wall Street knowledge. We understand what most people know when they are getting started. Most importantly, we also know what they don't know. We genuinely care about our readers. We want you to succeed, but first we want to teach you what we have learned so that you can avoid losing your life savings along with your self-esteem. We speak from our hearts to your soul.

This book is for the individual who is interested in beginning a trading career on a part-time basis. This step-by-step guide is meant to serve the needs of aspiring part-time traders who want to know if they could be successful at day trading and need detailed guidance on setting up their day trading business.

A day trader is someone who trades stocks repeatedly during the day, but rarely holds a stock overnight. The exception to this definition is the day trader who engages in "swing trades," which can include holding a stock overnight. Day traders do much of their trading in short time intervals of a few minutes or less. These trades are known as "scalps," and the trader is often taking $1/4$- or $1/2$-point profits on stocks that are experiencing momentum. Some day traders prefer longer trades: buying stock in the opening hours and holding for longer-term runs. This can include holding a stock most of the day and selling prior to the close. The typical day trader is making numerous short-term transactions each day. The day trader's needs are very different from the needs of a long-term investor.

You have read about day traders, watched TV specials about them, and wondered if you have what it takes to become a successful day trader. Your reasons for wanting to be a day trader may be varied—you may want to earn additional income, or perhaps your employer is going through continual downsizing and you are not sure if you may one day become a victim of this process. Maybe you have always wanted to be self-employed, to work from home, to set your own hours. No one can afford to risk his or her financial security, to give up current income, without first trading as a part-time trader long enough to become consistently profitable.

It is critical to make the transition to day trading by first becoming a part-time trader. *Day Trade Part-Time* provides a step-by-step approach. It will show you how you can determine if you are suited to day trading. It will show you how to set up your own day trading business on a part-time basis, and how to test your own day trading skills before you risk your precious trading capital.

This book was written to answer the most common questions about starting out as a day trader. You will see the risk and rewards of trading, and the pitfalls that capture and destroy many potential traders. Upon reading this book, you will know whether trading is for you. This book can cut months off your learning curve and possibly save you thousands of wasted dollars.

The information that takes most traders years to gather will be yours after reading this guide. Two years ago, there were only a few books available pertaining to electronic trading for the individual, and those books did not contain the real information needed to become properly educated. Now, with the proliferation of books, financial Web sites, and Internet trading rooms, you need a guide to filter the good from the bad. You will need to make many decisions regarding education, brokers, hardware, software, and Internet connections. These decisions should be made in advance of your commitment to go forward, to assure that you are headed in the right direction. Our tips will guide you through each of these decisions, letting you jump-start your trading. No other book that we are aware of does this for you!

Day Trade Part-Time is not meant to teach you all of the intricacies of trading. That process can take months, if not years, to accomplish. Our goal is to direct you to the best educational tools and equipment available to maximize your chances of succeeding as a trader. Most importantly, this book will show you why you need these tools and equipment. If you are currently trading, the resources provided should help you become a better trader.

This book does not teach theory. We emphasize the key elements of successful trading, such as enforcing stop losses, trading conservatively, and using an on-line trading room. We will give you a brief overview of the markets so that you will know your way around as you continue your education. Additionally, we describe with text and charts two simple bread-and-butter trading strategies: a short-term momentum trading strategy and a consolidation-breakout trading strategy. With these strategies you will have the basis to develop a trading plan that will maximize your chances of becoming a successful part-time trader.

Finally, we have introduced the ultimate simplification system, **SureStart**, to reduce the information overload a beginner may experience. The sheer volume of decisions required before you can even begin simulation or paper trading can easily overwhelm you when you are new to trading. You will need to make major, expensive decisions before you are ready to do so. The **SureStart** suggestions in this book will simplify those decisions. These suggestions are opinionated, concise recommendations on specific choices for everything you will need to get started trading. We give you our best choices for brokerages, trading sites, educational programs, and much, much more. These are our personal choices, with detailed reasons for these choices. These recommendations let you simplify your early trading preparation by implementing a totally defined and tested program as indicated by our **SureStart** designations throughout this book. Over time, as your level of knowledge increases, you can adjust these choices for your own personal trading style.

If you want to become a successful part-time trader, you must be fully prepared. To help you succeed, we wrote this handbook from the heart and from our trials and errors over the past two years. We share our experience of day trading with you to help you avoid the many pitfalls of trading that we endured. Our guide, with its **SureStart** suggestions, will get you properly started with the material all other books seem to ignore. We will walk you through the numerous decisions that you must make before you can even place your first trade. We get you there and beyond. So, jump in now and find out if you, too, can become a successful part-time trader.

JOHN COOK
JEANETTE SZWEC

Sacramento, California
Wilmington, North Carolina
August 2000

acknowledgments

We would like to thank Claudio Campuzano, Assistant Editor, John Wiley & Sons, Inc., for his support and guidance throughout the completion of our book. We owe a special thank-you to author Richard Beatty for his help and encouragement in getting our book published. We thank Judie Healy for her outstanding efforts in developing our Web site. We thank Dan Allen for his insights and suggestions and Jo Spier and CyBerCorp Inc. for use of their charts. To Eva Harvey we extend thanks for her support and many hours of proofreading. A thank-you to Linda Askew for her comments on our early draft and her encouragement throughout the process of preparing this book, and to Ellen Rickert for her guidance every step of the way. Special thanks to family and friends who have given so much support and tolerated lack of communications. With a special thanks to Drs. Joe and Nancy Czarnecki, Mary Szwec, Elaine Fowler, and Cricket Roginson.

And finally, a very special thanks to our sons, Zach Cook and Mike Jankowski, for their patience when we had deadlines to meet. We also thank both of you for the joy you give us every day of our lives.

J.C.
J.S.

about the authors

John Cook

Traders come from many different professional and experiential back grounds. For myself, prior to day trading, I was the department head of general claims, The Western Pacific Railroad Company (now merged with the Union Pacific Railroad); president of a product development and marketing company; and partner in a multi-family development company.

I first bought and sold stocks after college. I began day trading full time in mid-1997. Starting to day trade without guidance was very painful to me both financially and emotionally. Not knowing where to get trained and educated, cost me many thousands of dollars in travel, hotels, and lost income during the time I was not employed. Beginning my trading by using one of the common on-line brokerage firms cost me literally thousands of dollars because of delayed order executions. I was trying to be a trader, but I was using a broker that was not suited for active day trading.

My training began with a day trading course in New York City taught by Marc Friedfertig and George West, the authors of *The Electronic Day Trader* and *Electronic Day Trader's Secrets*. This was followed by a month-long course taught by Jea (Jay) Yu, the author of *The Underground Level 2 Daytrader Handbook*. This was supplemented by a software orientation course in Austin, Texas, given by CyBerBroker.

When I started using the appropriate software for active trading, I did not stick with simulation trading as long as I should have. Why? Because I had used too much of my capital paying my monthly bills while trying to prepare for trading without the proper guidance. Thus

I felt that I had to trade live as soon as possible to start earning a living. So instead of simulation trading and learning at no risk to my capital, I learned by trading live and further depleting my capital. Eventually I recovered, but it was a long, hard road. This is more than a personal story; it is the path that most day traders have traveled.

I am earning a living from my home as a professional trader. Additionally, I have used my experiences to co-develop a seminar for part-time traders.

Jeanette Szwec

We sometimes get to trading by very strange, circuitous routes. I was a single mom who hated anything and everything to do with stocks. I couldn't read a paragraph about stocks without being bored to tears. So how did I get into day trading?

I spent most of my career as an executive with a Fortune 500 company, primarily in consumer marketing assignments. In the last few years with that company, I was transferred to a small town on the North Carolina coast and became quality manager in a large manufacturing organization. The company was going through downsizing programs every one to two years, leaving every employee stressed and miserable. So, in 1996 when it announced another downsizing, I decided to request early retirement and left the company where I had been employed for 27 years. The manufacturing plant was located in a town with virtually no jobs—more of a resort community. I knew I could not get another decent job without moving out of that town, but I had promised my son when we moved there that I would not move again until he finished high school. So here I was—a single mother, unemployed, no job prospects in mind, and living off my savings. Not a pretty picture economically! I decided to spend my time learning about stocks in order to maximize my investment income since I would be using that income for living expenses until my son graduated from high school. I hated reading about stocks and I hated everything to do with investments, but I dove into it anyway.

A friend jokingly said I should try day trading. At that time, I didn't even know what day trading was. I started searching the Internet for information on day trading, found a few trading rooms, started getting free trial memberships. After a few months, I was totally hooked. My initial hatred of all things dealing with stocks and investments was converted into a fascination of all things dealing with day trading. Unfortunately, I didn't know who to go to for advice. I had no idea about who was giving me good advice and who was giving me bad advice. I had no ability to differentiate between expenditures that were critical (like signing on with a brokerage specializing in day trading) and expenditures that were wasteful (the list here would be much too long). So I started my day trading learning curve by doing one stupid thing after another.

I had a large on-line discount brokerage account that I thought would work for day trading. I had heard some people in a trading room talk about other kinds of brokers, but they never explained it well enough to convince me I needed them. Remember that I was living off my limited savings, so the thought of spending $300 a month just to have a more sophisticated brokerage seemed like a huge waste of money. Little did I know that trying to actively day trade at a standard discount broker was actually the biggest waste of money. Order executions were slow. Every time I wanted a current stock quote, I had to go through a long process to get it, and I could never get a quote up on the same screen as that needed to place an order. Plus, I couldn't use the same money to trade the same stock on the same day—a major disadvantage here. This is one of the definite limitations of trying to trade in an investment account.

When I wanted to join a trading room, I didn't know who to ask to find out which trading room was good. When I wanted to learn day trading, I had no hint of where to go. Who was honest? Who knew what they were talking about? Confusion reigned. And every mistake I made was financially devastating. Each day I didn't make money was another day that I was not only depleting my savings but also eroding my self-confidence. It was clear that the process of getting into day trading was difficult: a maze of paths with no clear direction or approach. For a single mom who was financially strapped, learning to day trade without direction was something I could not afford.

After months of research and of trial-and-error trading, I am pleased to say that I have successfully developed a strategy that allows me to earn a comfortable living as a professional day trader. I am also co-developer of a seminar for part-time traders.

contents

chapter 1

day trading as a business

day trading, a business, not gambling

Why is day trading looked upon by some as gambling? Probably because there are many people with little or no experience who are trading stocks on a daily basis. Undoubtedly they start their trading with no plan. These people are, indeed, just gambling with their money. They may make money for a while, if they are lucky, but they soon start losing money and never recover. We are sure most of these people are wannabe day traders, trading from a browser-based online brokerage. They have no basic concept of how to be successful at day trading.

Anyone who starts a business is faced with a risk of failure. The more preparation you do, the less risk you take, and the better your chance of success. Is starting a business a gamble? Yes, it could be. However, if you have researched, prepared, and been trained or guided by someone in the business that you are entering, then you are minimizing your risks. You are taking calculated business risks, not gambling.

Still, starting any business is speculative. Success is not guaranteed. Many factors influence success and you may not have control over all of them, so it is best to be well prepared and properly capitalized. You prepare your business so that the odds are in your favor to succeed.

You must approach part-time trading as you would any other business, with as much effort and research as it would take to build any successful business. It requires long hours and hard work. As in any other business, success doesn't come easily or quickly. Patience and time build your business.

If you envision becoming a part-time trader, you must devote the time and effort needed to develop this business completely. We suggest you begin a careful process of preparing yourself for the business of day trading stocks part-time. Some of you will later expand your business into commodities and futures contracts. Others may become full-time traders. The proper equipment, education, and sufficient simulation trading will be the foundation of your business. Our **SureStart** suggestions will serve as the experience of others helping you along the way.

When you open the doors to your new business, you will pay close attention to detail. You will begin by making trades in which the odds of a successful trade are very much in your favor. However, you will need patience to take advantage of these favorable trades. We will show you the importance of discipline, and we will share with you key analytical tools to aid in your trading. If you practice that discipline and use those tools, you can become a successful trader. Is this gambling? We think not.

pitfalls of trading

We must start with a word of caution. Trading is very difficult to master successfully. Trading is complex, not only because of the scope of what you must learn, but also because of many other factors involved. We want you to know that we did not write this book to encourage you to trade. Our book will show you the risks and rewards of trading. It will also explain what it takes in time, commitment, education, equipment, and dollars to become a consistently profitable part-time trader. If you decide this is what you want, you will have the information necessary to achieve that goal in the most expedient and effective manner.

Trading, like any other business, has its share of failures. In fact, it has a high percentage of failures, with estimates ranging from 70 to 80 percent. Please remember this when you make your decision about whether you should trade or not. Trading is a zero sum game. A zero sum game is like a game of musical chairs, one player takes from another; one wins and another must lose. In this business of trading, you are up against the best professional traders, market makers, and even powerful institutional investors.

For most traders, including the authors of this book, a major hurdle in trading is controlling your emotions while trading. Discipline is critical. You may say to yourself, as we once did, "Emotions? Not a problem for me." Prepare to be surprised!

When emotions are in charge, logic and objectivity are left at the front door. Your anxiety kicks in. The charts and data seem to be running faster than they did when you were paper trading. You are no longer viewing the charts with the same calmness and clarity as you did when paper trading. The larger your share size, the more anxiety!

We hope you are beginning to understand that emotions make trading very difficult. Fortunately, we have many tools and technical analyses available that will allow you to see the markets objectively, and to trade with confidence, not with your emotions.

Additionally, you can paper trade or simulation trade for however long it takes to master the technical analysis techniques you want to use. You will build confidence in your trading skills by paper trading. You can then move into live trading with the same confidence by using small share lots. With this approach, your logic, not your emotions, will control your trading.

In the section titled "Your Trading Account and the Learning Curve" in Chapter 6, you will see what can happen if the learning curve begins poorly, as in our example of Trader I. Total disaster! Fortunately, our Trader II (later in the chapter) took a different path leading to success as a part-time trader.

In Appendix B, you will find an article on day trading prepared by the Securities and Exchange Commission, Office of Investor Education and Assistance. Although written primarily for full-time traders, we strongly suggest that each of you read this article. It covers many of the risks associated with trading, particularly for those traders who have not followed the path of discipline and education.

SureStart ⟩ suggestions

This book was developed by professional day traders who have gone through the trading start-up process the hard way and decided that there had to be a better, more efficient approach to getting started. Now you do not have to subject yourself to the trial-and-error method of becoming a part-time trader.

For those of you who wish to start learning and trading as soon as possible with maximum efficiency and while optimizing the use of resources, we have supplied recommendations in each section of this book that are designated by the words **SureStart**. Our **SureStart** suggestions for products and services are very opinionated and were selected because they are used by a number of professional traders, including ourselves. All of our **SureStart** suggestions are applicable to you as a part-time trader. You can use them to get started as soon as your schedule allows. For each item, we give you our personal reasons for making this item our **SureStart** recommendation.

You should read and review everything we recommend in this manual before you commit funds to anything. You must feel comfortable in what you are doing. Remember that while the **SureStart** suggestions work well for many of us, some of them may not be suitable for you or for your trading style. For example, there are a number of brokerage companies covered in this book. CyBerBroker has been given the **SureStart** designation in two categories. However, you may research others and find that another brokerage company is more suited to your needs. So research all the options in each section, determine the benefits and usefulness to you, and then make your decisions. We offer this guide as a suggestion. It is up to you to make the final choice.

chapter 2

part-time trading

the benefits of part-time trading

If you are presently a full-time employee or are running your own business, we strongly suggest that you start as a part-time trader. In trading circles you will hear people say, "Don't quit your day job to trade."

Being a part-time trader is good for many reasons. After reading this book, you will have a substantial list of decisions that you need to make, including decisions on hardware, software, and education. You can make these decisions in your spare time while continuing your current career. In part-time trading there is no pressure on you to be profitable immediately. This will allow you to be more focused on your preparations, education, and live trading. You won't feel the burden of needing to replace your previous, full-time income in order to meet your daily expenses.

While learning to trade, losses will inevitably occur. These losses could diminish your working capital to a point where it is difficult for you to make sufficient profits to offset your trading expenses. Because you are a part-time trader and are still earning an income from another source, you can continue your present lifestyle despite these early losses. After examining the cause of your losses and taking corrective action, you will be able to replenish your trading capital and resume live trading. If you are sustaining losses on a regular basis, you should return to simulation or paper trading until you are consistently profitable. Always protect your capital!

Without the pressure of having to earn a substantial amount of money, a part-time trader can start live trading conservatively using small lots of 100 to 200 shares. This will substantially lower your risk compared to trading in lots of 1,000 shares. Never forget that all traders make losing trades, so be prepared for this. With a small number of shares, the losses you incur will be relatively small as long as you keep tight stop losses on your losing trades. We will cover stop losses in detail later in this book.

Once you are a successful part-time trader with monthly profits that exceed your present employment income, you may consider full time trading or you may be very comfortable continuing as a part-time trader. Remember: Your success as a part-time trader may be partially related to the fact that you can focus on your trading because you do not have to worry about replacing an established income.

different approaches to part-time trading

Your approach to part-time trading will be as individual as your fingerprint. No two part-time traders operate in exactly the same manner. We will show you a variety of approaches that can be used, but only you can choose the exact approach that makes the most sense to you.

prime-time trading

It is not necessary to sit in front of a computer for the entire day. There are some hours distinctively better for trading than others. Some part-time traders work just in the morning hours. Some split their day, trading in the first few hours after the market opens and then again in the last 90 minutes before the market closes. Others place trades shortly after the open and then close out their positions at the end of the day. As you can see, there are many variations in trading methods and rationales for each.

What hours are best for trading? The prime-time hours are between 9:30 A.M. and 12:00 P.M. EST and again from 2:00 P.M. to 4:00 P.M. EST. During these hours, the volume of trading is greatest, offering the trader the most liquidity and usually the greatest price fluctuations. Liquidity and volatility are the most important essentials to traders. Additionally, during the morning hours the market makers usually have their hands full handling order flow, and they may not be as interested in playing games and hiding their true intentions from other traders.

Part-time traders on the West Coast have a distinct advantage over their East Coast counterparts. They can trade before going to their full-time job, and again during their lunch hour. These trading times would be 9:30 A.M. to 12:00 P.M. EST (6:30 A.M. to 9:00 A.M. PCT) and 2:00 P.M. to 4:00 P.M. EST (11:00 A.M. to 1:00 P.M. PCT).

Between 12:00 P.M. and 2:00 P.M. EST, trading is slow and there is a lack of volume. This results in less liquidity in a stock, particularly in the less frequently traded stocks. As a part-time trader you must be very cautious during these hours. In these slow hours you may buy a stock and then notice it's starting to turn down. You may want to get out, but you can't find anyone to buy back your stock, except at a much lower price. Not good.

If you choose prime-time trading hours, remember that your top priority is to protect your full-time income. Don't give your employer any reason to terminate your employment. If possible, bring your own portable computer to work and use your own ISP. Trade on your own time, such as your lunch hour. When you start this activity, your goal is not to generate an immediate income from trading; your goal is to learn how to trade. So, when you are on your own time, like your lunch hour, start by tuning into a trading room, following the stock prices, watching charts, and doing simulation trading. Eventually, you can transition to real-time trading during this same time period.

who can be a part-time trader?

The one thing we can't do is to teach you how to be a part-time trader without spending some time in front of your computer during the trading day. As a part-time trader doing either short-term momentum trades, consolidation-breakout trades, or even one to five day-swing trades, you are going to be an active trader and will need to find some way to spend time trading during the New York business day. Chapter 5 will explain these strategies in detail.

Many professions or occupations lend themselves naturally to participating as a part-time trader. Some professionals, such as doctors, lawyers, or dentists, have the ability to set their own schedule in a way that allows some time each day for trading or they can set one weekday aside for trading because they may need to work on a weekend day. This natural scheduling is an excellent way for them to participate as traders while maintaining their current professional status.

In addition, many full-time workers do not work standard schedules. Numerous service people need to work on the weekend and have a compensatory day off during the week. Others are on four-day, 10-hour day schedules. Others work evenings or have nontraditional schedules that again allow them to regularly participate during the standard trading day at least one day per week.

In addition, there are numerous retirees or people phasing into retirement who still maintain a traditional income stream but have blocks of time available to trade during the New York business day. Many of these people are able to supplement their retirement income by phasing out of their traditional jobs and are viewing trading as a potential new income opportunity. They are excellent prospects for becoming part-time traders.

If you can only trade for a short time during one or more trading days a week, you need to know how to best use those hours. We have developed a section in this chapter, "Trading by Time Zone," which will give you some idea of the best way to use your trading time based on where you are located in the world. We divide the New York business day into subsections and describe the type of trading that is best in each of those subsections. We then combine that information with the typical hours you may have available for trading based on a typical workday in your time zone.

be flexible

Some of you will not be able to trade during the workday in your current job, so trading while protecting your *current* income may not be a viable option. This is the point where you must make some tough decisions. Are you ready and willing to change jobs? Can you get another source of income? Can you find a job with more flexibility? Is shift work available so you can devote some time during the prime trading hours to develop your trading skills? Are flex schedules available?

Some of you will be able to rescue some of the prime trading hours by taking advantage of flexibility in your current position but others may find yourselves stuck with no flexibility at all in your current assignments.

Still—*do not quit your day job*! We suggest a transitional approach. Use your vacation, even accumulated sick time, to create some day-trading hours. Four weeks of vacation could be turned into almost half a year of day trading one full day a week. If you can take your vacation in half-day increments, you would have 40 weeks of experience using one-half day a week to trade.

Don't give up your day-trading dream! If you really want something, you will find a way to make it happen.

overnight plays and swing trading

Despite your best efforts, some of you will not be able to trade for one or more hours during the trading day. Does this mean that you have to give up your dream of part-time trading? No way! You can still build up an income stream by choosing a different approach to trading.

Our approach until now has been to find time to be a pure day trader—looking to trade in short time intervals of a few minutes or less. This type of trader, also called a scalper, is looking for one-quarter to one-half point profits by capitalizing on a stock's momentum. This trader needs to be present for a sufficient period of time during standard market hours to capitalize on these momentum plays.

However, another approach that will work for the part-time traders who have less flexibility is *swing trading*. In swing, or position trading, a trade is held overnight or for several days. Swing trading is an outstanding route for the part-time trader. With swing trading, you can devote just minutes a day to executing your carefully planned trades. In our discussion of trading-room sites, we cover two trading rooms that have an excellent performance record in calling stocks for swing trades. One Web site (www.mtrader.com) is particularly good for suggesting stocks that might go up overnight. The moderator's calls are made in the last five to ten minutes of the standard trading day. These stocks can be sold premarket, and your trading day can be over before the official markets have even opened. The other Web site (www.swingtrader.net) is excellent at calling stocks for swing plays that can be held for one or more days. After the stock meets the criteria for entering the trade, it can be held for several days without constant monitoring. Additional information on these Web sites can be found in Chapter 7.

If you want the best training for swing and position trading, you can't do better than a program given by Top Gun Trading. For details, send an email to tgtrading@uswest.net. More on this in Chapter 4 in the section, "Setting Up Your Educational Program."

Remember, you may only spend a few minutes executing a swing trade, but this does not mean that you only devote minutes to your trading business. Overnight holds are inherently risky. You must know your stocks, understand their history, and be using a sophisticated strategy to choose your purchases. If you think this is easy money, you will become a loser. This is not gambling; it is a business requiring time, skill, and study, and the longer you plan on holding the stock, the higher the risk. Preparation and caution are needed here, but swing trading can be an excellent approach for the part-time trader with limited time available during standard market hours.

new trading hours

The times, they are a-changin'. Market hours have traditionally been from 9:30 A.M. to 4:00 P.M. EST for transactions on the NYSE, Nasdaq, and AMEX exchanges. Most traditional brokers and online brokers have only permitted stock transactions for their retail customers during these hours. Yet daily on CNBC, you hear stock prices quoted both before the market opens and after it closes. What is this and how does it affect your career as a part-time trader? To understand this, you need to be familiar with electronic communication networks (ECNs) and how these ECNs are changing the way stocks are traded. Institutional investors have had the ability to buy and sell stock outside of standard market hours by using self-contained, fully automated ECNs. These ECNs are alternative routes for placing stock orders. They give a trader access to selling stocks outside the normal Nasdaq and NYSE routing, but they also allow for trading of stocks both *before* and *after* standard market hours.

Large institutional investors have used Instinet before and after hours to trade stock after significant news events have occurred. Instinet is an ECN owned by Reuters, and it is the largest of the ECNs. When earnings reports have been released either before or after market hours, large institutional investors have been able to capitalize on this news by having instant access to trading those stocks. When earnings announcements are made after market, you hear CNBC correspondents talk about how the stock is trading up or down on Instinet.

Until recently, trading on these ECNs was limited to large institutional traders and a small number of day traders that use sophisticated brokerage companies that gave access to trading on ECNs. This included brokerages such as CyberBroker and MB Trading. Depending on the particular ECNs offered by these brokers, trading was available at these brokerages through ECNs for before and after standard market hours. The exact length of time varied by the ECN and by the brokerage companies.

These before- and after-hours trades through ECNs were very advantageous to the savvy trader who knew the tricks and risks of before- and after-hours trading. It was also hazardous to those who tinkered in this arena without sufficient knowledge about the dangers of buying when liquidity is limited.

But *major changes* are occurring for retail customers of standard online brokerages. With each passing day, more standard online brokerage firms are announcing their intentions to make after-hours trading available to their retail customers.

Where will this eventually lead? Will we be trading stocks 24 hours a day? Time will tell, but the trend is clear. Trading hours are getting longer; volume will increase in before- and after-hours trading, thereby increasing liquidity and the ability to sell something you already bought.

But *you*, the part-time trader, will be the beneficiary. If you choose to specialize in swing or position trades (trades which are held overnight or for several days), you will have extended hours for trading and less need to trade during your standard workday. Liquidity will be increased with expanded volume, so the corresponding risk of trading in off hours will be reduced.

We want to offer one word of caution to anyone new to off-hour trading. As with anything relating to day trading, there are huge possible rewards and equally huge risks. Market makers like to play with the unsophisticated trader; they can post any price with essentially no risk because they have no obligation to buy or sell stock at their quoted prices either before or after market hours. Lots of games are played here! Lots of danger lurking for the trader who is not aware of the pitfalls of trading during off hours! Don't get caught in these traps! Study. Do research. Learn. Discuss. Do not play in this playground until you know the rules.

As a part-time trader, you can participate in off-hour trading with the big guys, but you must be extra cautious. Stay in the game. Be smart. Don't get caught in traps. Be a survivor, not a loser in the day-trading game.

trading by time zone

In most of our discussions, we talk about trading hours by referring to the New York business day trading hours, which are 9:00 A.M. to 4:00 P.M. Eastern Standard Time. Let's take some time to look at the trading day in a variety of locations around the world. We will first observe what the natural trading hours are in locations around the world, and then put together a suggested list of strategies to follow during various time segments of the trading day. Keep in mind that many countries switch to Daylight Savings Time in April, and this switch can change the time difference for those countries that do not participate in Daylight Savings Time.

Selected Locations		Hour Difference from NYC Trading Hours
New York City, New York	0	9:30 A.M.–4:00 P.M.
Chicago, Illinois	–1	8:30 A.M.–3:00 P.M.
Phoenix, Arizona	–2	7:30 A.M.–2:00 P.M.
San Francisco, California	–3	6:30 A.M.–1:00 P.M.
Honolulu, Hawaii	–5	4:30 A.M.–11:00 A.M.
London, United Kingdom	+5	2:30 P.M. –9:00 P.M.
Paris, France	+6	3:30 P.M. –10:00 P.M.
Geneva, Switzerland	ı6	3:30 P.M. –10:00 P.M.
Perth, Australia	+13	10:30 P.M. –5:00 A.M.

If you are involved in an occupation that requires your presence during standard work hours of 9:00 A.M. to 5:00 P.M., there are certain time zones from which it will be easier for you to trade either before or after work. In Hawaii, you can participate in most of the trading day before leaving for your day job. In Western Europe, you can also participate in much of the trading day, but most of your participation will be after the first few hours of the market day, assuming you are working standard business hours. However, you may be able to trade during your lunch break if you have the traditionally longer lunch often enjoyed in European countries. We have been told that many Europeans like to trade in the U.S. stock market because of their belief that there is far greater availability of information on U.S. companies, and that this information is less costly to obtain.

As you consider which hours you will be able to trade, you must consider what type of activity and trading strategy works best in different time segments. There are times in the day that are more appropriate for our **SureStart** short-term momentum trading strategy, and there are other times that are best for our **SureStart** consolidation-breakout strategy.

There are some hours during which you should just watch and

not trade. We will review all these time segments, using the New York business hours as our guide.

segmenting the market day

Certain hours of the day are better for certain strategies than for others. As a part-time trader, you may only have a few hours a day available to do your trading, so it is critical that you understand how to use your hours effectively. The times in this guide are all quoted in Eastern Standard Time. You can use the previous table to convert these hours to your local hours. Times are approximate and the time segments may overlap. We assume that you would not be trading during all these time segments but that you are trying to choose which segment will be best for your chosen trading strategy. In this write-up we refer to the short-term momentum trading strategy and the consolidation-breakout trading strategy. These are discussed in depth in our chapter on **SureStart** trading strategies.

premarket: 8:00 to 9:30 a.m.

During the premarket time segment, there is less liquidity in the market and it can be difficult to exit positions. We prefer to limit premarket activity to selling positions that were held overnight in anticipation of a gap. If a gap does occur, the gap is often at its peak around 9:15 A.M., so this is generally a good time to sell those positions. Premarket is not a good time to enter new positions since this is a time that market makers can be manipulating stock prices.

9:30 to 10:00 a.m.

This is an excellent time for using the short-term momentum trading strategy. Stocks that have gapped up (opened above where they closed the previous day) will often lose that gap during this time. Stocks that gapped down will often reverse slightly to fill part of that gap during this time. There is a lot of momentum in the market during this time segment. Moves can be strong. You must excel at execution before you start trading during the first half hour of the trading day. If the market volume is particularly heavy, there is also a tendency for quote data to lag in this time period, which further increases the danger of trading during this time.

If you plan to trade consolidation breakouts, you can use this time to make a list of stocks that either gapped up or were rising strongly at the open. You will then scan charts of these stocks all day long to identify their consolidations. Consolidation breakouts are discussed in depth in Chapter 5.

9:40 to 10:20 a.m.

This is known as the reversal period. Whatever direction the markets were taking at the open, they tend to reverse direction during this time. If the market was rising sharply at the open, expect a pullback during this time period. This is also an excellent time segment for experienced short-term momentum traders to be scalping the reversal, but for newcomers the best use of this time is to scan the market for strength stocks. These are stocks that were moving up strongly at the open, and now are holding their own while other stocks are falling during the reversal period. This strength is always relative, but you want to find stocks that are not reversing or that fall less than other stocks. These stocks will be good to play when you are going long using either the short-term momentum trading strategy or the consolidation-breakout strategy, both discussed in Chapter 5. This is a great time to be looking for these stocks that have high relative strength. Relative strength ratings can be found in *Investor's Business Daily*.

10:20 to 11:00 a.m.

This is another excellent time for scalping if you are using the short-term momentum trading strategy. There is still a great deal of volume in the market, and the volume brings momentum into the strong stocks. If you are using the consolidation-breakout strategy, this is an excellent time to be scanning the strong stocks you previously identified to determine if they are in consolidations.

10:45 a.m. to 12:00 p.m.

This is our favorite period for playing morning consolidation breakouts. All the scanning and chart watching you have done all morning will pay for itself during this time.

If you are using the short-term momentum strategy, you will also be looking for the lunchtime reversal that occurs fairly often. As in the early-morning reversal, stocks that have been moving up into this time period will often go through a sharp reversal during this time. Sometimes this occurs at 11:30 A.M., sometimes at noon, and sometimes it doesn't seem to occur at all, but keep your eye on this because it can be a great opportunity for scalping.

12:00 to 1:00 p.m.
Go to lunch. This is not a time to be trading. You can only get into trouble. This is the time the market makers play games with inexperienced traders.

1:00 to 3:00 p.m.
This is the best time for playing afternoon consolidations. You have been scanning stocks all day, watching strength stocks to see if they are continuing upward, and watching charts to find which ones are consolidating. These are the hours where the afternoon breakouts are most likely to occur.

2:00 to 4:00 p.m.
Short-term momentum traders should return from lunch around 2:00 P.M. This is when the volume returns to the market, and with its return comes the momentum plays. It is critical to trade this strategy when there is sufficient volume in the market.

3:30 to 4:00 p.m.
During this time, swing players decide if there is a stock worth holding overnight in anticipation of a sharp increase overnight. If the market is strong at the very end of the day and if the individual stock is at its day's high at the very end of the day, you need to decide whether to buy and hold the stock in anticipation of a gap occurring the following morning.

Other swing players that are already in a trade will use this time to decide whether the risk/reward relationship is strong enough to hold their stock overnight or whether they should exit their positions before 4:00 P.M.

So, part-time traders, pick your favorite trading strategy, find a block of time where you can trade that strategy, and get started on your training. We will be giving you lots of resources for developing your skills and learning the essentials of trading. Don't rush it. Take your time and do it right. Protect your money and your peace of mind.

deciding not to trade

When you are finished with this book, some of you may say that this is all too complicated, too risky, too costly, too time consuming or just too early in the day to get up. On a positive note, by reading this book, you will have answered your question of whether or not you want to trade. Now you can move on to something else if you elect not to trade.

enjoying your success

With time and patience and good judgment, many of you will start to gain confidence in your trading abilities. You will see profits—not on every trade, but on a high percentage of them. You will have kept your losses to a minimum by implementing a tight stop-loss procedure. You will have become a successful part-time trader.

Enjoy your success, build up your trading account, and buy yourself something with your profits. But don't be too quick to quit your day job. The market is one of cycles. You can have a technique that works beautifully for three months, and then doesn't work at all for the next three months. Be sure you are consistently profitable through a variety of cycles—bullish, bearish, technology strong, and technology weak—before you move to full-time trading. You will get there, but get there with a minimum of stress and a maximum of profits by taking it slow and steady and not rushing into this transition.

chapter 3

key concepts
for day trading

market exchanges

Materials furnished in this section provide you with a very general overview of how the different markets function, particularly the Nasdaq (National Association of Securities Dealers Automatic Quotation) stock market. By knowing how these markets work, you will understand why you will need certain education, hardware, and software to make yourself competitive as a trader. There are two other principal markets: The New York Stock Exchange (NYSE) and The American Stock Exchange (AMEX).

NYSE

The NYSE is an auction market where a specialist oversees all transactions for the particular security that he represents. The specialist will establish the current public best bid and offer for the stock. This is done on the NYSE trading floor or via the electronic SuperDOT system, which is the electronic way of matching and executing orders in a quick and efficient manner. The auction model works best if the buy and sell orders are somewhat matched. On particularly heavy trading days, executions may take minutes or a stock may be halted if order imbalances occur.

Specialists are also required to provide liquidity in a stock when there are no current bids or offers in the market for the stock they represent. The specialist, out of necessity, becomes a buyer of stock on the way down and a seller of stock on the way up.

Only the best bid and best ask prices are displayed on the computer quote screen for NYSE stocks. Designed only to give stockbrokers a general indication of a stock's current market, these are known as *Level I quotes* (or the *inside bid* and *inside offer*). The main thing to remember about trading in the NYSE is that the specialist is in control, not you. The specialist is the only one who knows what all the other bids and offers are that were presented to him. Brokers and traders only see the best bids and asks (the Level I quotes). This is why the NYSE is sometimes referred to as a nontransparent market. As traders, we do very limited trading in NYSE stocks as compared to the Nasdaq.

Nasdaq (formally known as the Nasdaq Stock Market)

Unlike the NYSE, Nasdaq is not an auction market and it has no specialist through which all transactions pass. The Nasdaq allows multiple market participants, such as market makers and ECNs, to place their names on a list of buyers and sellers and to trade through an electronic market linking buyers and sellers worldwide. Liquidity is provided through the participants themselves and trades are instantaneous. Unlike NYSE stocks, Nasdaq quotes are transparent because all bids and offers by market makers and ECNs can be seen (the Level II quotes). Level II quotes display all the bids and all the offers (asks) and the actual size of those bids and offers from every market maker in a particular stock. In addition, the inside bid and ask are always the top line on the quote screens. These let you know what all the market makers are doing with a particular stock at the exact same time. By viewing the different price levels you get a quick picture of a stock's support and resistance levels. Support and resistance levels are covered in the section on trading strategies in Chapter 5.

The Nasdaq quote screens can give you the immediate trend in a stock by the movement of bid and ask prices. Additionally, you can see support and resistance levels developing. Furthermore, we traders can post our own bids or offers on an equal basis with everyone else through an ECN of our choosing, or we can post a bid or ask price between the spread (the difference between the inside bid and the inside ask price).

Only in the past few years have Level II displays become available for use by the general public, usually through other brokers that specialize in electronic day trading in Nasdaq securities. This is very essential if you are trading momentum stocks for one-quarter- to one-half-point gains.

how Nasdaq works

In order to understand the Nasdaq market, you need to know about market makers and ECNs.

market makers

Market makers are independent brokers/dealers who represent and execute their clients' orders, usually institutional investors, through the Nasdaq electronic trading network. Market makers collectively provide a market in securities, because they are required by Nasdaq to be both the buyers and sellers of the stocks in which they are making a market. If a market maker is willing to sell, then he must also be willing to buy at a reasonable price at the same time.

As an individual trader you are not only competing against other traders with years of experience but you are going head to head with the best market makers in the world who handle their customers' order flow. Just knowing their own customers' order flow gives market makers a tremendous edge over other traders by letting them see the potential trend in the market. If a market maker has a million shares of Dell to sell for his client, he knows the price in that stock will likely be going down due to the sale of this client's order. We as traders do not have that information. Additionally, market makers trade against you with the firm's funds for the sole purpose of making money. Companies such as Merrill Lynch (MLCO), Salomon Smith Barney (SBSH), Bear Stearns (BEST) and Goldman Sachs (GSCO) all act as market makers.

Fortunately, with experience in watching the Level II Nasdaq quote screen on your computer, you will get a feel for those times when a market maker has a large seller of shares, and you will also be able to discern when he is done selling.

ECNs

ECNs are independent electronic trading systems that allow market makers, institutional investors, and private individuals to trade Nasdaq stocks. All ECN bids and offers are posted on the Nasdaq computer network which links buyers and sellers around the world.

Instinet

The largest ECN is known as Instinet. Its symbol on Nasdaq is INCA. Until recently, Instinet was primarily used by investors and market makers. However, day-trading brokerages are now starting to offer direct access to Instinet to their customers. As more market makers have started using Instinet, we traders have more access to liquidity by being able to buy and sell to them when the symbol INCA appears on the Nasdaq quote screen.

Island

The second largest ECN is known as Island. Its symbol on Nasdaq is ISLD. This ECN is inexpensive and broadly available. As traders we can access Island through electronic brokerage firms who provide this access through their trading software. See Chapter 4 for availability.

Once a trader places an order through Island to buy or sell shares, Island will first attempt to match the order with what is in the Island system. If not immediately executed (and we are speaking of milliseconds here), the order will be posted worldwide on Nasdaq quote screens as an ISLD order. Through Island, you can become a market maker as an individual trader. If you place an order between the spread, you are making new market for that stock at that moment with a new bid or ask price.

Island provides maximum liquidity to traders along with speed and reliability. Additionally, just as Nasdaq quote screens show all the buy and sell orders, Island also has its own buy and sell order quote screen that can be accessed by some trading software. As with Nasdaq screens, you can see the immediate trend in a stock by viewing the movement of bid and ask prices on Island. The best bid and ask price posted on Island is the price posted on Nasdaq Level II under the symbol ISLD. There is an exception to this. If a trader indicates that he does not want his Island bid or ask displayed on Nasdaq, it will not be. This can prevent that bid or ask from crossing or locking the markets if it is higher than the Nasdaq inside bid or lower than the Nasdaq inside ask. Bidding or offering through Island is the choice of many traders for entering and particularly for exiting a trade. This is so because of the liquidity offered through the Island.

Other ECNs
Other ECNs are not as large as Island. These will show up on Level II under these symbols: ATTN, ARCA, REDI, NTRD, and BTRD. More ECNs are on the horizon, so be prepared to see many more.

other routes for trade executions
SOES (Small-Order Execution System)
The Nasdaq small-order execution system, SOES, is designed for quick executions of small orders of up to 1,000 shares. It is a mandatory system requiring a market maker to buy on the bid and sell at the ask. This system is based on a first-come, first-served basis. Also there is an allocation of time between refreshing bids, that is, the time allowed to honor the next buyer or seller at the same price or to adjust his quote to a new price. The bottom line to all of this, as traders, is that when a stock is moving fast, only a few will get out by a SOES order, while the rest must wait in line. By the time you finally get out, the stock may have moved a point or more against you. However, SOES can work well with slow moving stocks.

SNET (Selectnet)
Selectnet is a system in which market makers can communicate electronically with one another. The market makers can bid or offer stocks to each other over this system, and these bids do not show up on Nasdaq screens. Selectnet is not a mandatory system. Traders, through an ECN, for example, can indicate a preference to a market maker to

trade at that market maker's quoted price but the market maker is not obligated to fill the order. In reality, your order would only get filled if it were to the benefit of the market maker.

understanding a Nasdaq Level II quote screen

The Level II quote screen is also known as the stock box or the market maker box. The stock box is one of the most intricate and sophisticated tools within an electronic software program. Not only does it display in real time all Level I and Level II data, but it can also be changed by the trader to customize various execution features. From the stock box, the trader will be sending and canceling orders. On some software programs, more than one Nasdaq stock box can be viewed simultaneously.

The Level II stock box (see Figure 3.1) displays the following:

1. The stock's symbol such as CSCO.
2. The price from yesterday's close: $59\frac{1}{16}$.
3. The price at the open: $59\frac{3}{16}$.
4. The tick direction: up indicates bid has increased; down indicates bid has decreased.
5. Level II: The market maker/ECN, the price, the share amount, time of trade.
6. The current share size trader is attempting to buy or sell: 1,000.
7. Tier Limit View: SOES tier limit on a stock (T10 = 1000, T5 = 500) (see note following this list).
8. The last trade: 59.
9. The share size of last trade: 1,000.
10. The change on the day: down $\frac{3}{16}$.
11. The ratio: Ratio of market makers/ECNs at the bid vs. ask.
12. The volume (Cumulative shares traded on current day): 4,277,700.
13. Time and sales + Scrolls through time and sales data.

figure 3.1   Level II stock market box

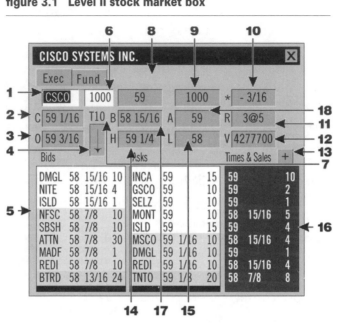

14. The high for the day: $59\frac{1}{4}$.

15. The low for the day: 58.

16. Time and sales: Displays all trades in real time. Multiply the share size displayed by 100 to get exact amount of shares traded.

17. The current bid: $58^{15}/_{16}$.

18. The current ask: 59.

Note: The tier limit is the maximum lot size allowed for SOES execution. A tier limit of T2 is a 200 share limit on SOES executions.

chapter 4

preparing to trade

setting up your educational program

Our suggestions for your educational program will include a list of books, trader training courses, and educational Web sites. Our most important learning tools will be two Web sites: (1) www.underground trader.com and its trading room, The Trading Pit, for short-term momentum trading, and (2) www.swingtrader.net and its trading room for consolidation-breakout trading.

books

We have listed the books in the order that we think would be most beneficial to you as a part-time trader. We assume that you will also be watching an educationally oriented on-line trading room and reading material from its seminar archives. We will discuss this later in detail and give our recommendations.

SureStart > *The Electronic Day Trader,* Marc Friedfertig and George West

We feel this is the best book for learning about electronic execution systems. It has excellent coverage of alternative trading strategies. Excellent overall coverage of day trading.

SureStart ▷ *The Disciplined Trader,* Mark Douglas
Controlling emotions and maintaining discipline is the focus of this book. This is the key to success as a trader. Start reading this book now. Then reread it. Once you start trading, you will really appreciate what is being said in this book.

SureStart ▷ *Technical Analysis Explained,* Martin Pring
The book gives excellent, comprehensive coverage of the field of technical analysis. It explains price patterns, moving averages, stochastics, and many other technical indicators. It is a must for all traders' book shelves.

Japanese Candlestick Charting Techniques, Steve Nison
This need not be the first book on your reading list, but once you start simulation trading and are feeling comfortable with using candlesticks as your charting tool, start reading this book. Then read its sequel, described below. This is a very detailed book on charting with candlesticks and the meaning of the candles. Charting with candlesticks is perhaps the most popular method of charting used by traders. Once you understand the information furnished in a candle you will understand why it is so important for your trading.

Beyond Candlesticks, Steve Nison
This is somewhat of a repeat of Nison's first book, but definitely an expansion and, therefore, necessary reading.

Electronic Day Trader's Secrets, Marc Friedfertig and George West
This is not a necessary book, but it is inspirational and informative after you have traded for a while.

Reminiscences of a Stock Operator, Edwin Lefèvre
This, too, is not a necessary read, but it is fun and somewhat historical. Originally published in 1923. This book is as relevant today as it was when it was written particularly because it applies to the reading of the tape, which would be similar to watching today's Nasdaq Level II quotes. It is widely read.

day-trading training courses

Training courses come in a variety of formats: CD-ROMs, on-line courses, and live classes.

Some live classes are given in different city locations and some are at permanent sites. Classes may vary from a few hours to 20 intensive days of all-day training. Prices range from $49.00 to $6,000.00.

We certainly recommend stretching you training budget as far as possible. Good training will be the foundation of your trading. The difference between proper training and poor or insufficient training could mean the difference between success and failure as a part-time trader.

You will learn a great deal by choosing an educationally oriented on-line trading room. However, to get you started sooner and more efficiently, and to help you qualify for opening some electronic brokerage accounts, we strongly suggest that you start with one of the courses covered in the following paragraphs. We recommend that you go to each Web site and see what is offered, where it is offered, when it is offered, and the course pricing. Part-time traders should consider scheduling a course during your vacation time.

We are not giving a **SureStart** recommendation for a training course because we have personally participated in only two of these trading courses. For this reason, we feel it would be unfair to give a **SureStart** suggestion here. We have reviewed the course providers' outlines. In some cases we have spoken to their representatives and have selected some that merit your consideration.

In reviewing all the course materials, there appear to be many fine courses available. We know that some of you may feel much more comfortable learning in a classroom environment with a computer screen and instructor in front of you. So carefully check out each Web site listed below to see what is offered. If you choose a live class, ask what software is used. If given a choice, we suggest CyBerTrader software or RealTick, in that order, because this is the same software used by many electronic brokerage firms.

There are three levels of courses. The best would be those courses that provide classroom settings with instructors, live data feeds, and, in our opinion, CyBerTrader software (because of its capability to let you simulation trade). A second level of instruction will have you training on-line at home. No other special software is required—only your computer with the basics. This may be the way to go for some of you. The third level would be a CD-ROM course. Naturally, the cost for each type of training is substantially different.

During the initial learning phase, it is very important for anyone considering part-time trading to sit in front of a CyBerTrader or RealTick screen and see how this software works. You can do this by going on-line to www.cybercorp.com and using their trading simulator for CyBerTrader. This service uses the previous day's data and is available 24 hours a day. And it's free! A great way to get familiar with this sophisticated Level II software program.

Courses, promotions, and prices may change. Please use the information given as a guide to what is available. Always check the training Web site for their most recent information on pricing and course availability.

Taking a trading class will give you a head start in your learning curve. It may also improve the likelihood that a brokerage firm that uses sophisticated software such as CyBerTrader or RealTick will approve you for a new account. Before actually taking any of the listed courses, we recommend that you check with your preferred brokerage firm and ask them if the training course that you are considering qualifies you to open an account with them.

The training courses listed below are in alphabetical order by the name of the school or company that offer the courses:

Bandit University (www.banditu.com)
Guerrilla Trading Course. The cost is all-inclusive and ranges from $3,000 to $5,000 for the week. This includes all equipment, and data feed and a detailed proprietary manual. It is available with modules for front-end software and execution packages, including CyBerTrader and Townsend Analytics (RealTick). Courses are given throughout the United States. Other training/coaching is available. See the Web site for further details.

The Momentum Trader (www.mtrade.com)

MTrader Interactive Day Trading CD-ROM Course. Price $149.00.

Self-Paced On-line Day Trading Course. Price $49.00.

On-line Trading Academy (www.on-linetradingacademy.com)
Two major courses are offered:

One Week On-line Trading Boot Camp. This course uses CyBer-Trader or Executioner trading software. See the Web site for detailed class outline. Price: $3,000. This course is a prerequisite for the 10-day On-line Trading Immersion Course. Teaching facilities are located in Irvine, California. On-the-road training courses are also available. Check the Web site for details.

Ten-day On-line Trading Immersion Course. This course uses Cy-BerTrader software. See the Web site for detailed class outline. Price: $3,000. If you sign up for both courses, the fee is reduced to $5,400 for both courses. You can space the courses apart if you wish. The course fee can be credited to you on a per-ticket basis through several brokerages including Momentum Securities, Inc., www.soes.com and Cy-BerBroker, Inc. www.cybercorp.com.

Based on the course outlines, we believe that you will receive a good foundation for your trading if you complete both courses. You will be well prepared for simulation trading, and you can continue your training in an educationally oriented on-line trading room.

A training cost of $5,400 plus accommodations, travel, and approximately 20 days of your time may seem like an expensive way to learn day trading. However, courses such as these two will accelerate your learning curve and should be well worth it, if this cost falls within your budget for education.

Several other less extensive courses are available. Please check the Web sites.

The Pristine Day Trader (www.pristine.com)
Pristine offers three trading courses:

Pristine's One-Day Seminar, nine-hour intensive, interactive workshop. Price $995.00.

Pristine's Three-Day Seminar, nine-hour intensive days, interactive workshop. Price $3,500.00. (Taught by Pristine's CEO and co-founder Oliver L. Velez.)

Pristine's Two-Week Seminar. Kirkland, Washington. Price $3,500.00

The three-day seminar is taught at Pristine's corporate headquarters in White Plains, New York. Other seminars, including the one-day seminar, are taught in various locations around the country. The software used is The Executioner, which is RealTick based. Seminars include a detailed 125-page course book for future reference.

There are several major benefits to opening an account with The Executioner following the completion of Pristine's three-day seminar. You will be eligible for $3,000 worth of credit towards your course registration. Executioner will discount your commission fee by a full $5.00 per trade on your first 600 trades, and you will receive a $600 credit towards a subscription to Pristine's Real Time Trading Room. See the Web site for other benefits and detailed course descriptions. While at this site, we suggest you read and study the excellent free educational material under Education.

Top Gun Trading E-mail (tgtrading@uswest.net)
Highly recommended! Top Gun Trading specializes in teaching people how to trade intermediate-term trends in stocks and the market, specifically, day trading, swing, and position trading. The class covers the use of market indicators, options, and technical analysis. The instructors show how to trade in all market environments, what to look for to catch the big moves in the hottest stocks, and how to generate a steady income using stock trading as a vehicle for financial security. Teaching the use of trading software is not a part of this instructional program. Classes are taught by two top-notch swing traders, Garth Doverspike and Brooke Englishe. Approximate cost $2,500. E-mail for class schedules and costs: tgtrading@uswest.net

Tradersedge.net Seminars (www.tradersedge.net)
This five-day course is given live in New York City. Price: $1,695. A $400 discount off the seminar price if you open an account with Broadway Trading LLC.

Marc Friedfertig and George West, authors of the books *The Electronic Day Trader* and *Electronic Day Trader's Secrets*, teach the course. One of the authors of this book attended this course approximately a year-and-half ago and felt that it was excellent. The course uses software called the Watcher. At the time we took the course, no use was made of computer-generated graphs. The course is an excellent beginner's course for the money, with loads of synergy coming from Marc, George, and the traders at Broadway Trading LLC, located on the same premises, 50 Broad Street, New York City. If you choose not to trade on the Watcher system after taking this course, you will need to educate yourself on the use of other software such as CyBerTrader or RealTick. Please view site for course details, scheduling, and other information.

Trading Places Inc. (www.trading-places.net)
The Official Level II Study Guide. This is an on-line, electronic publication, available for registered users only. Cost $249.95. See the Web site for details.

The UndergroundTrader (www.undergroundtrader.com)
The Underground Training Home Study Package. This home study package can be viewed in full HTML as an interactive Web site installed on your desktop computer, which is accessible off-line at your convenience.

This course is definitely for traders. It covers the reality of day-to-day momentum trading. This course will be most useful if you have had some prior experience with trading software such as CyBerTrader or RealTick. Although this course will not teach you the use of these two software systems, it may be ideal for those of you with some trading experience who have trading accounts with Level II data and charting capabilities.

The original live version of this course is no longer offered. Price of the self-study course is $750.00 and includes a 30-day trial membership to the Trading Pit and access to all archives of past seminars and logs. Trading consultation via e-mail with instructor/author Jea Yu is included, as well as with instructor Ral Lockhardt, Ph.D.

Other Day-Trading Training Courses
We have furnished you with a variety of the trader training courses offered. A good source for additional courses available would be Cy-BerCorp's Web site, www.cybercorp.com. Look under Trading then Investor Resources.

evaluating and choosing an on-line trading room
We believe that the ongoing commentary and educational resources provided by the following trading Web sites and their trading rooms will be the most significant source of your initial and continual education. These trading rooms want you to be successful, and they are inspired to provide you with meaningful information so you will continue using their services. We personally believe that the moderators of these particular trading sites are genuinely concerned for their members and provide as much support and education as possible.

A trading room should provide you with the following:

Ongoing education

News alerts: premarket and during market hours

Analysts' upgrades and downgrades

Market and sectors trends

Suggested trading calls and the reasons why

Cautionary advice

Experienced traders sharing knowledge of trading

Archives of trading logs are a real use to the part-time trader. The part-time trader can benefit greatly from the fact that some of these sites, including The UndergroundTrader and The Momentum Trader, archive the entire log from their daily trading room sessions. By reviewing these logs, you can bring yourself up to date on the day's market activities and on any educational commentary presented during the day.

We have given the **SureStart** designation to three trading rooms, each for a particular trading style that you, the part-time trader, may adapt. Read the write-ups of the two different trading strategies in Chapter 5, and choose your trading room to be compatible with your preferred trading strategy. Additional trading rooms are also listed after the three **SureStart** recommended rooms.

 The UndergroundTrader
This is our **SureStart** recommendation for Short-Term Momentum Trading.

The Web site for The UndergroundTrader, www.undergroundtrader.com, and its related trading room, The Trading Pit, are two educational tools available to those interested in intraday trading of momentum stocks. This is where you are going to learn the specifics about profiting from price volatility and trends. Jea (Jay) Yu, a highly successful professional trader, operates and hosts this site. Jay is extremely good at teaching via commentaries while he calls trading plays in the trading room. Additionally, he and others from his staff, particularly Russell Lockhardt, Ph.D., known as Ral, host seminars during the New York lunch hour. Each day's seminar has been archived since the inception of the trading room. For us knowledge-seeking traders, this provides an unbelievable amount of educational material available for reading during the off-market hours.

Some quotes from Jay from the logs of July 29, 1999, pertaining to education:

The goal in the Pit is twofold

1. To give trade alerts that members can profit from.
2. To EDUCATE, EDUCATE, EDUCATE members to be self-sufficient.

An example of The UndergroundTrader's efforts to provide a variety of insights and to expand our educational horizon is Ral, the resident psychologist and a professional trader. Ral has a very unique trading strategy called the Three Point Break System, which many traders in The Trading Pit use with success. This system, which is very adaptable to different time frames, can work well for the part-time trader. Ral makes daily contributions to the trading room where he describes the movement of the overall market indices, such as the DOW, Nasdaq, S&P futures, etc. Additionally he makes many ongoing commentaries about the psychological aspects of trading. Ral also gives many outstanding seminars, which are logged in the archives.

The educational material at The UndergroundTrader is focused on short-term trading and the application of technical analysis to stocks that are showing volatility during the day.

There are important commentaries given by Jay and Ral all day long. By watching before the markets opens, you will see the value of the premarket comments made by Jay and other traders. This premarket report includes a list of stocks to watch for that day. Additionally, during the day, there are continual reports on news releases that could influence your trading. Once the market opens, there will be trading suggestions by Jay. In addition, Jay and Ral make live commentaries about the market, its trends, trading strategies, activities and moves of market makers, etc. Because Jay's trading strategies are based on various chart patterns, you must have software capable of delivering live charts in order to fully utilize his commentaries. From these charts and the analytical tools on the charts, you will see the reasoning behind Jay's commentary.

There is a one-week free trial for the site. However, the free week does not include access to the archives. To understand the full benefits of the site we suggest that you start watching it at least one hour before the markets opens, or 8:30 A.M. EST. The seminars are usually given between noon and 1:30 P.M. EST and are archived, thus enabling a part-time trader to share in these valuable educational lessons, even if they can't be present live.

The cost of being a member of The UndergroundTrader's trading room, The Trading Pit, is $250 monthly. This is approximately equal to the profit from one momentum scalp trade.

A good time to join this trading room would be after you have opened a trading account, are up and running with your trading software, and are ready to do some simulation trading or paper trading. You should definitely have live Level II quotes and live charting. You will be able to follow the trading calls from The Trading Pit on your screen and watch how the charts reflect a stock's movement. From this room you will hone your skills and develop your trading style. Additionally, you will be continuing with your educational process through Jay and Ral's commentaries.

The UndergroundTrader is the Web site that ties it all together: the archived educational material, ongoing commentaries, seminars and real-time trading. Trades in The Trading Pit are not based on intuition but on technical analysis and definitive time charts. This gives you the ability to review and understand the basis of each trade. This is an excellent learning tool from a credible source!

SureStart > *The Momentum Trader*

This is our **SureStart** recommendation for overnight gap plays. Overnight gap plays are also referred to as overnight holds. A stock is bought at the end of the trading session in anticipation of its opening higher than the price at which it closed. This "gap" in price is the potential profit for this strategy.

The Momentum Trader is a trading and educational site started in 1979 by Ken Wolf, professional Day Trader and author of the book, *Momentum Investing*. This site is perhaps the best-organized Web site available and focuses on a proprietary trading method called High Percentage Momentum Methods. We encourage you to visit the site for a full understanding of this method. The site location is www.mtrader.com.

This trading Web site has several different trading rooms specifically geared to particular types of traders.

The educational program is extensive: running commentary in the trading rooms, dedicated classroom time with Ken Wolf from 12:30 P.M. to approximately 1:30 P.M. EST, evening classes and more. An on-line day-trading course is available for $49.00 and their CD-ROM day-trading course is $149.00. Additionally there is a lot of free educational information provided at this site. The cost of membership to this site is $200 per month. The membership includes an on-line day trading course. There is a free, one-week trial membership available.

Part-Time Trading. The Momentum Trader trading room is particularly interesting to part-time traders. Ken Wolf is the moderator and highly skilled at picking stocks that are good for overnight holds. Holding a stock overnight is potentially one of the most profitable strategies, but at the same time it is a strategy that is inherently high risk. Stocks often experience the majority of their movement overnight, but this movement can be in your favor or it can be your biggest nightmare. Therefore, minimizing the risk of this strategy and optimizing the potential for profitability is critical for part-time traders who want to use the overnight-hold strategy.

Ken has an outstanding track record of recommending stocks worthy of holding overnight. He carefully watches both the overall market action and the individual stock's performance both throughout the day and, most particularly, at the very end of the day. He has very strict standards that he applies before calling any stock as a potential for an overnight hold. His performance record on his calls is very impressive. Since his calls for stocks to consider for an overnight hold occur in the last few minutes of the trading day, and since you can sell the stock premarket, the part-time trader can employ this strategy while trading for only a few minutes at the end of the day, and for approximately 30 minutes premarket. Not a bad deal considering the potential profitability of employing this strategy.

A word of caution: you absolutely must simulation trade with this strategy before trading with your funds. There is risk. One of the authors held a stock overnight that was doing great at the end of the day (note: this was not a recommendation by Ken or this trading room). Before the market opened the next morning, an analyst stated that this $200/share stock was only worth $50/share. In the following five minutes, long before the market opened, the stock lost $50 per share in valuation. Oh, my! Not a good trade! With overnight holds, there is always the potential for some insanity to occur such as this. So, if you want to hold overnight, be sure you learn how to minimize your risk: use smaller shares, and learn from an expert, Ken Wolf.

SureStart *The Momentum Trader Swing-Trading Room*

This is our **SureStart** recommendation for the consolidation-breakout strategy. Stock prices do not go straight up or down. An up trending stock will go up, then level out for a while, then resume its upward movement. The opposite is true for a down trending stock. When the stock is leveling out, we call this the consolidation period. When a stock breaks out of its consolidation, we call it a breakout. Trading these breakouts is the basis for consolidation-breakout strategies.

This is a trading and educational Web site hosted by Toni Hansen and Brandon Fredrickson. This is the place to go for part-time traders interested in using the consolidation-breakout strategy. Toni and Brandon share the moderating and bring excellent calls to the room for both swing trades and consolidation-breakout trades. The site location is www.swingtrader.net

Although the swing-trade calls are excellent and based on strong technical indicators, we have given this room the **SureStart** designation because of its calls on consolidation breakouts since that is a featured strategy for part-time traders. However, if you have any interest in multiple-day swing or position trades, this room is outstanding.

We have been particularly impressed with this room for a number of reasons. Their track record is excellent, they definitely do their homework before giving a call. There is no hype, and no cyber locker room mentality here. There is a businesslike yet friendly atmosphere. There is an absence of high-pitched emotionalism. That type of emotionalism is dangerous. It can lead a newcomer to jump into a bad trade because too many people are claiming winnings, tempting a newcomer to enter questionable trades. (See the section on greed.) We have never seen this behavior in this trading room and that makes the room much safer for newcomers.

Toni and Brandon know when to give calls and when to sit back. If they feel the market is dangerous and unpredictable, they do not call any trades. This is outstanding! There are times that you should not trade and these moderators have the guts to stay silent and not make calls when the market is dangerous rather than lead people into questionable trades.

Another strong point of this room is the emphasis placed on money management. They never call a trade without specifying a *stop* price. Excellent discipline on their part and very beneficial to the new trader.

Toni generally handles the consolidation-breakout calls. She definitely does her homework in preparing for these calls. She analyzes the daily and intraday charts for trends and points of support and resistance. She takes great care when making a consolidation-breakout call in order to optimize its likelihood of being profitable.

And finally, Toni and Brandon give classes after the market closes on Monday and Friday. The classes are well done and continually reinforce the techniques used for their swing and consolidation-breakout calls. At a cost of $100 a month, this room is definitely worth its cost!

Linda Bradford Raschke Trading Site
Linda Bradford Raschke is a top trader. She was featured in Jack Schwager's book, *The New Market Wizards*, and more recently in Sue Herrera's book, *Women of the Street*. In 1995, she co-authored the best selling book, *Street Smarts*.

Information can be found at www.mtrader.com/linda.htm. This trading room describes itself as "real-time futures analysis and trading over the Internet. . . . our trading consists of a mixture of S&P day trading and short-term swing trading (1–2 days) in the futures markets."

Dialogue and commentary is posted throughout the day from Linda Raschke and Victoria Pearson. The membership fee for this room is $350/month. The room is open on the first trading day of every month for a free trial. A great chance to observe and decide if this format is for you.

The Pristine Trading Room
The Pristine site offers a high-quality trading room, The Pristine Trading Room, in addition to outstanding educational material. Details can be found at www.pristine.com.

Oliver Velez is the president of Pristine.com. He established Pristine as an educational site, making recommendations but also explaining when, how, and why to buy a stock. Greg Capra is cofounder of Pristine. Their trading techniques have been favorably mentioned in the *Wall Street Journal*, *The New York Times*, and *Barron's*.

According to their Web site, this trading room "provides live, ongoing stock recommendations and market commentary throughout the trading day . . . members with access receive a steady flow of real-time trading ideas . . . timely news items which can ignite trading opportunities are broadcast instantaneously. Breakouts and stocks that are on the verge of exploding to the upside are issued in a matter of seconds . . . Subscribers also receive premarket commentary moments before the market opens, and informative postmarket remarks are made to summarize each day's events." The Pristine Trading Room membership fee is $525 monthly. A free trial membership is available to see if this room meets your needs.

#DAYTRADERS

#DAYTRADERS is a free trading room that can be accessed through MIRC. Details of the site and directions for connecting can be found at www.daytraders.org (there is a minimal charge for AOL users to maintain a security firewall). Many members of other paid trading rooms also keep a window open to this free trading room. Although no one "expert" is in the room making calls or giving commentary, there are a number of topnotch traders who participate in this room and who announce calls and recommend trades. With a few private conversations and a little observation, you can get a feel of which traders you want to watch and follow.

This room is outstanding to watch before the market opens because there are hundreds of traders bringing news alerts to the room. Because there are so many participants, there is a wealth of information that can be obtained by tuning in before the market opens. Conversely, there is also a lot of clutter you must weed out, but with the free membership, this is definitely a place you should explore. Note this is not the same as Daytraders.com, which is a paid Web site trading room.

Summary of Web Sites for On-line Trading Rooms
Here, for a quick reference, are all the Web sites we've discussed:

SureStart www.theundergroundtrader.com

www.mtrader.com

www.swingtrader.com

SureStart www.mtrader.com/linda.htm

www.pristine.com

www.daytraders.org

selecting a brokerage firm

On-line brokers have their own proprietary software. Most allow trading on the Nasdaq, NYSE, and AMEX exchanges. In general, they only furnish Level I quotes for Nasdaq stocks. Some brokers have a continuous feed of live quotes; some have limited live quotes, and some only offer delayed quotes. With most on-line brokerage companies, the type of quotes you get is determined by what you pay. The best brokerages for day trading have proprietary software, which allows you to trade stocks by seeing the Level II quotes from Nasdaq. Even as a part-time trader, we recommend that you trade with Level II quotes unless you are primarily swing trading.

With most brokerage firms offering Level II quotes, you need to trade 100 or more times a month in order to have the service fee waived, and this fee can be as high as $300 a month. Although fees are coming down, we recognize that some part-time traders will not trade often enough to have fees waived. In that case, you may wish to trade with a more traditional on-line brokerage firm that only provides Level I quotes. If you don't have Level II quotes, you will need to adapt strategies that can work with that reduced level of sophistication in quote information.

brokerage firms offering Level I Nasdaq quotes

Examples of on-line brokerage firms that offer Level I quotes are Schwab, Fidelity, and Ameritrade. Gomez Investors is a Web site that lists and rates brokerage firms offering Level I quotes and is well worth looking at if you are interested in only Level I quotes. Gomez rates brokerage companies in different categories and by type of investor. Other firms that have rated on-line brokerage firms are Smart Money, Barron's, and Forrester Research. Please note that these firms rate none of the electronic brokerage firms using sophisticated high-performance software.

SureStart Our **SureStart** designation, CyBerX, is not rated by any of the aforementioned firms. Neither is MB Trading's MB Lite. These new entries were designed for traders that are more active and they are not yet included in ratings of the more conventional on-line brokerages.

CyBerX offers its Level I quotes using a Windows-based application, versus the Web-based browser system used by other on-line brokers. There are many advantages to using a Windows-based application, such as faster executions, real-time tick charts, instant trade confirmations, all trading information on one screen, and more.

Considerations in Selecting an On-Line Broker
In making a decision about choosing an on-line broker, consider these features:

Speed of execution

Speed of page confirmations

Site down time

Timing out on a Web site

Number of screens needed to execute a trade

Real time charts

Can you place stops on Nasdaq orders?

Up-charge in commission rate on Limit Orders vs. Market Orders

After hours trading. Hours available; what ECNs are utilized

Are live quotes available on your execution screen?

Live or delayed graphs

Are options available?

Free news services

How quickly can you reach a broker on the phone in an emergency?

Are you protected from executing orders beyond your margin?

Ease of understanding daily and monthly statements

Securities Investors Protection Corporation (SIPC) insured

Is live customer service by phone quickly available?

There are several Web sites that rate stock brokerage firms according to categories, such as ease of use, customer confidence, onsite resources, cost of services, and so on. Two such Web sites are Gomez Investors www.gomez.com and Smart Money www.smart money.com.

The five on-line brokerages with the highest market share that offer Level I quotes are listed here:

1. Charles Schwab (www.schwab.com)
2. E*Trade (www.etrade.com)
3. Waterhouse (www.waterhouse.com)
4. Datek Online (www.datek.com)
5. Fidelity (www.fidelity.com)

brokerage firms offering Level II Nasdaq quotes

Examples of electronic brokerage firms having Level II Nasdaq quotes are CyBerBroker and MB Trading. Additionally, some of the traditional on-line brokerage firms such as E*Trade and Fidelity are now offering Level II quotes or will in the near future. Details on these brokerage firms can be found on their respective Web sites.

We have chosen to feature CyBerBroker and MB Trading in this section because of the level of service they offer specifically for the active trader. They utilize two different software programs: CyBerBroker uses CyBerTrader and MB Trading uses RealTick. Most other electronic brokerages use either CyBerTrader or RealTick software.

CyBerBroker and MB Trading have representatives present in several Internet trading rooms. They are available in the trading rooms and on separate support channels so that any trading-room member who is experiencing a problem with their execution system can receive help immediately. We have been impressed with the customer service of both CyBerBroker and MB Trading and feel comfortable in suggesting these two firms to prospective part-time traders.

Both CyBerBroker and MB Trading allow orders to be executed outside of standard market hours using ECNs. This will be very advantageous to the part-time trader.

SureStart *CyBerBroker*
CyBerBroker has its own proprietary software, CyBerTrader, and it uses Penson Financial as its clearinghouse. Please check CyBerBroker's Web site, www.cybercorp.com for requirements in opening an account. Requirements will include minimum initial trading capital, net worth, and trading experience. While at the Web site, check out data service and commission costs.

Two years ago, one of us had the opportunity to be one of only 50 people to attend a trading seminar sponsored by CyBerCorp (the parent company of CyBerBroker). This trader was very impressed with the staff and the CEO of CyBerCorp, Philip Berber. The staff is very customer oriented. No matter how many questions we still ask, there is a smiling and willing person at the other end of the telephone ready to help. Their technical support staff is extremely knowledgeable.

Once you have a funded account at CyBerBroker you have unlimited use of simulation trading using live data and the functions of CyBerTrader software. This is a distinct advantage in using CyBerBroker.

We chose CyBerBroker for our own trading for the same reasons we have chosen them as our **SureStart** suggestion: CyBerBroker is the home base of CyBerTrader software; their server systems are reliable; they allow unlimited use of simulation trading that realistically duplicates real-time trading; there is no extra charge for futures data; longer trading hours are available than with other brokerages; there is direct access to Instinet; they provide excellent brokerage assistance if you need it; options are available.

MB Trading
MB Trading, Inc., is a branch of Terra Nova Trading, LLC, and all transactions are through Terra Nova Trading, LLC. MB Trading uses Real-Tick software supplied by Townsend Analytics. RealTick software is available through other brokerages, but we have featured MB Trading because of their commitment to customer service. Please check the MB Trading, Inc. Web site, www.mbtrading.com, for account requirements, services, and fees.

MB Trader offers Turbo Options, a sophisticated quote system displaying real-time options prices, including strike price, root, monthly expiration, and open interest. Many traders that start off trading securities eventually move on to options, so this feature is very important for the more experienced trader.

Whether you choose CyBerBroker or MB Trading, you will have an excellent system and outstanding customer service. Please visit each Web site and review the material so that you can decide if one of these brokerages is more suited to your needs.

Remember, account requirements, services, and fees can change. Always check on these prior to opening an account.

Here is a summary and quick reference for you:

CyBerBroker, Inc. (CyBerTrader www.cybercorp.com)

MB Trading/MB Trader (www.mbtrading.com)

Other Electronic Brokerage Firms Specializing in Level II Quotes
For a complete list and brief description of practically all the electronic brokerage firms specializing in active day trading, check out this Web site: www.investorlinks.com. These are a few others:

1800DAYTRADE.COM (www.1800daytrade.com)

A. B. Watley, Inc. (www.abwatley.com)

The Executioner (www.executioner.com)

Momentum Securities, Inc. (www.soes.com)

Polar Trading, Inc. (www.polartrading.com)

Brokerages Offering Entry Level Software for Level II Quotes
Please note that the software with Level II quotes in this category
does not have the sophistication of the software previously listed.
However, CyBerX 2 could be an excellent choice for part-time traders
trading less than 50 tickets (buy or sell) per month. CyBerX 2 has all
the advantages of CyBerX with the additional advantage of integrating
Level II data. Visit the respective Web sites for complete details. Here
are a few sites to consider:

CyBerBroker's CyberX 2 (www.cybercorp.com)

E*Trade (www.etrade.com)

Fidelity Investments (in the near future) (www.fidelity.com)

MB Trading's MB Custom (www.mbtrading.com)

selecting Level II trading software

In making decisions about choosing Level II software and its support-
ing company, consider the following:

Reliability of service

Ease of use

Detailed instruction manual available

Quality of charts and the analytical tools to use with them

Number of charts available

Number of Level II screens available

Quality and availability of technical support

Ongoing training programs from the software provider available

Training programs offered by third party vendors

Active research and development team involved

Options available

Free news services available

Protection from executing orders beyond your margin

software specializing in Level II quotes

Most brokerage firms specializing in Level II Nasdaq quotes use either CyBerTrader or RealTick software. Therefore, we will focus on these two software programs. Please realize that we cannot detail all the features of these two software programs. For more information, we suggest you visit each site.

SureStart ⟩   *CyBerTrader*
CyBerTrader software was developed as a proprietary product by CyBerCorp and is available from them. This is a very sophisticated software system that includes decision support "alerts," charting and technical tools, timing tools, dynamic stock screening capabilities, execution systems, position management, account management, P&L and trading status, and Level II data. We have been particularly impressed with the vast array of decision support systems uniquely available in this software. These include intraday high/low breakout alerts, 52-week high/low breakout alerts, personal and dynamic graphic tickers that show the combined effect of price changes and market-maker activity on selected stocks in an easy-to-see graphic format. In addition, the full Island book is available as well as direct access to Instinet—two important ECNs. The open trade manager gives you a graphic representation of the status of all of your open trades. This is extremely helpful when you have had a partial execution on a sell order and need to be warned that you still have a partial position in a stock.

You can execute most order entry or routing commands either from your keyboard or with your mouse in the Level II stock box or in the execution control panel. All these functions are easy to use.

A unique feature to CyBerTrader is CyBerXchange. This function will basically do the thinking for you to get the best possible price and entry or exit. Depending on your trading strategies, these functions could be very helpful to you.

In addition to these unique features, CyBerTrader includes the capability of simulation trading using live data. (See our section on "Simulation Trading" later in this chapter to understand the true importance of this feature.) This feature will simulate trades on both

Nasdaq and the NYSE. It is very realistic—orders can be set to fill randomly or to fill consistently. With random fills, a new trader will experience the frustration of their order not being filled, much like it occurs in live trading. Additionally, the trader is able to practice entering both long and short positions in stocks with a realistic representation of real-time trading.

The importance of simulation trading should not be underestimated. It is probably the most important feature a new trader will use. It is far more realistic than paper trading and can help new traders familiarize themselves with the variety of routing and execution systems within the software.

The functions of CyBerTrader are very extensive, but with time and simulation trading, you can master it. Traders will eventually develop their own selection of favorite features to suit their individual trading styles. Some will use only a small fraction of the available features while trading. The selection of features and the speed of execution are awesome.

We have been very impressed with the continual improvements that are being made to the software. With Philip Berber's insights into the future of on-line brokerage operations, and the company's large research and development staff, CyBerCorp will continue as a leading electronic brokerage firm for the foreseeable future.

To see the full capabilities of this software, go to the CyBerCorp Web site. There is an on-line demonstration of CyBerTrader as well as a tutorial on the use of their software.

We have chosen CyBerTrader for our own needs for the same reasons we have chosen it as our **SureStart** suggestion: continued R&D in their innovative trading software; reliability of their software; excellent technical support team; the outstanding simulation trading mode that duplicates real-time trading; access to the full Island book and direct access to Instinet; a vast array of decision support tools and execution key functions; real-time risk-management tools; 80 stock-screening criteria to choose from, static or updated every 15 seconds!

We suggest you visit the site www.cybercorp.com/comparison. html for a detailed comparison analysis of the tools offered by CyBerTrader vs. RealTick.

Townsend Analytics RealTick
Our experience with RealTick has been through MB Trading. To understand the scope of RealTick software, we suggest you visit the MB Trading site as well as the Townsend Analytics Web site at www.taltrade.com

RealTick has many of the same features as CyBerTrader—full access to Level II, instant executions on Nasdaq, executions on NYSE, charting, market minders, and a large variety of other features. Real Tick offers excellent charting capabilities. The charts are easy to read, to size, and to enlarge the critical data you are most interested in. Time of sales (TOS) data is also easy to view on MB Trader. You can pull up the prior day's TOS data, which is interesting to do if you are studying historical patterns.

Please visit each Web site and review what is offered in each software program so that you can decide if one of these software systems is suited to your needs. Here is a summary of Web sites for quick reference.

CyBerTrader (www.cybercorp.com)

MB Trading (www.mbtrading.com)

Townsend Analytics (www.taltrade.com)

strategy for using an on-line trading room for short-term momentum trading

Once you have selected an on-line trading room, you need to have a plan about how you will use it.

First and foremost, a trading room should provide live ongoing education in the form of commentary from the host. This would include information about why trends are developing, why certain stocks are moving, how to interpret the graphs of different stocks in real time, and why certain stock trades are being called.

initial learning phase

During your initial learning phase, when a host calls a stock pick, go to that stock and look at the graphs and at the Level II stock box. Try to understand why this stock has been called. The host may say something about a stock prior to the call to support his choice. At other times, he may find a stock that is gaining in momentum and may immediately make the call without further information. Due to the volatility of trading these momentum stocks, the host may not have time to explain why he has recommended this stock, but usually will discuss the reason for the call after the call has been made. The reason may be a volume breakout, a stochastic bounce, or some other reason. Your goal here is to learn and to understand why a stock was chosen.

In the learning phase, do not start trading stocks that are called in a room. Just watch. Do not think that you can make money while learning. Trust us here; many of us have found out the hard way. It doesn't work. Learn from our experience.

While you are in your initial learning phase, don't even try simulation trading. In the excitement of the simulated trading, you will miss seeing the action on the charts and stock box. You must keep observing all the data and listening to the host so that you can learn how and when to get out of that stock. As your learning progresses, you can start simulation trading. However, start off right. When the host calls a trade, bring that stock up on your stock box and charts. Analyze it. See if you can understand why the host made the call.

Look at all the data in front of you: the S&P futures, the one minute graph, the five minute graph, the stock box with Level II quotes, and so forth. This may take you five to ten seconds, but in time, you will be able to make these decisions considerably faster. Decide if this trade makes sense to you. Perhaps it is a very fast-moving stock and for this reason, you decide not to enter this trade. Fast-moving stocks are dangerous to play even for the experienced because they can turn against you very quickly. Perhaps the spread, the difference between the bid and ask, is too wide—one-half point or more. This presents more risk when exiting a trade that goes against you, because you could easily lose one-half point if you had to exit quickly by selling at the bid. Now you find yourself already down one-half point, and you are just beginning your exit process. At other times, the stock could just be too expensive for your portfolio.

Just because your growing experience helps you identify a call as a good one, you still may not personally feel comfortable with entering the call. For instance, some of us love to play breakout calls on volume; some of us do not. Some of us feel more comfortable and have had better personal success playing one-minute stochastic reversals.

Many of the momentum stocks move exceptionally fast, both up and down. You will see many new traders in a trading room asking, "How do I enter and exit these fast moving trades?" The answer is skilled order routing and execution. Listen to the host's answers and practice them diligently. When a stock turns against you, time seems to speed up dramatically. You cannot waste time wondering or thinking how you are going to exit a trade. It is very important to practice this skill before you need it. You will need automatic reflexes on your keyboard or with your mouse. Keyboard executions can generally be made faster than those with a mouse. For those of you scared by the thought of using a keyboard, please know your keys can be color-coded and labeled to make things easier.

Moving from simulation trading to live trading is a very exciting experience. Now you are facing the element of emotion in each trade. Keep it in check. Easy to say, but hard to do. Keep in mind what you did in simulation trading and what brought you success. We suggest you start off in small lots of 100 or 200 shares. Trade slower-moving stocks, like CSCO or AMAT, and not fast movers like AMZN or YHOO. Until you have the experience of live order routing executions on slower-moving stocks, do not buy these fast-moving stocks in a live mode.

Remember that you are now trading live. Treat all the host's calls with caution. It is not that his calls aren't good. They may be great for some traders, but not good for your style of trading. They may involve more risk than you want to take. So go to each call, analyze what you see, and decide on your own whether to trade.

A trading room is usually flourishing with activity and excitement. This can entice you to overtrade. Overtrading can lead to impetuous decisions resulting in losing trades. Remember that when you are trading live, the bottom line is your profit-and-loss statement each day, week, and month. So, trade carefully and profitably.

As you progress, use the information that is given in the trading room to help you achieve the best results for your style of trading. Don't be a crowd follower. If you follow the crowd, you will probably remain stagnant in your educational growth. Who is to say that the best host, in any trading room, will be there the next day to guide you? Grow as a trader. Be successful on your own.

simulation trading

Before you can fully benefit from simulated trading, you will have to develop some trading strategies and rules. You may already have trading strategies but perhaps you will need to learn some new ones that are more applicable to day trading. Later in this book, we give you our **SureStart** short-term momentum trading strategy and **SureStart** consolidation-breakout trading strategy—two strategies to practice on your simulator. Practicing these strategies in simulation mode is the key to minimizing your financial risk as you learn to day trade.

paper trading without simulators

Paper trading: trading without having your funds at risk. Sound like a good idea? Yes, it is a very good idea and one that we recommend until you are the most proficient paper trader on the face of this earth!

First, decide if you are willing to pay the current inside ask. To make it as real as possible, trade no more than 500 shares at a time. If the price stays at the inside ask for 20 seconds, write down that you have made your purchase at that price. If the price did not stay for 20 seconds, repeat the process until you have gotten a price to hold for that length of time.

To sell, pick a price on the inside bid and let that be your selling price. If the price stays at the inside bid for twenty seconds, consider that you have made your sale at that price. If the price did not stay for twenty seconds, repeat the process until you have gotten a price to hold for that length of time. This is simple, fairly representative of real trading, and it is easy to do.

As a refinement to this, if you have Time of Sales (TOS) on your screen, you should watch to see how many fills were made at your price. To determine whether you would have gotten filled, compare how many fills were made versus the number of shares at the inside ask or bid at the time you made your paper trade, depending on whether you were buying or selling. If there were fewer fills on the TOS than those offered at the inside ask or bid, then do not count your paper trade as completed. You probably would not have gotten filled in live trading either. Be honest: You are only answering to yourself.

Now if you wish a much more elaborate and probably significantly more accurate paper trading method than the one just suggested, we suggest that you go to the About.com Web site at www.daytrading.about.com and find Rob Rak's excellent three-part series on paper trading. You can find this article by going to the "So You Wanna Be A Trader" series, Part III, and find the links, or search "paper trading." While you are there, read the wanna be articles. Very good!

trading with live data simulators

Simulation trading is an essential part of the trading learning curve. By practicing simulation trading, the part-time trader will learn how to apply different technical analysis and trading strategies to their stock picks. You will become familiar with routing and executing your trades so that you will be able to do so without hesitation. You will establish a trading plan and rules, which will test and tighten your discipline. Most importantly, you will practice these elements and develop confidence in your trading skills without risking your trading capital.

A word of caution: Some of you will experience sitting in front of a trading simulator as a world of fantasy. You will marvel at what you see. You will just want to start hitting the keys or clicking the mouse: buy, sell, buy, sell. This is getting off to a bad start! Remember that this is your part-time business. This is serious stuff. So once the dazzle has worn off, read and study your manual and learn the software. The sophisticated software programs such as CyBer-Trader and RealTick can do amazing things, but it takes time to understand how to use this software. Allocate the time and learn it from A to Z.

At first, practice entering orders not to test your trading skills but to test your knowledge of the software. Learn how to apply analytic tools such as stochastic indicators, moving averages, Bollinger bands, etc. To get the full benefit of simulation trading, first get educated on the trading techniques you want to use as a part-time trader. A good way to do this is by reading recommended books, watching videos, watching an educationally oriented trading room, or attending a trading course. This is the mechanical part of trading and you're fortunate you can learn it on a simulator.

simulation software

Practice your simulation trading on the same software you will be using for live trading. The best simulation software will use a live-quote feed and will execute your orders using a demonstration or DEMO account. All the bells and whistles of the live trading software should be up and running in the simulation software.

Many electronic brokerage firms offer some form of simulation trading. Brokerages vary widely on the length of time they will allow you to use their simulation trading software. Be very thorough in finding out what limitations and costs are associated with your broker's simulation trading. Be sure that you can do simulation trading using live data. Also, be sure that you are getting a simulation trading system, not just some canned demonstration program with limited data and watered-down trading software that may only allow you to trade Nasdaq Test-A and Test-B stocks.

Even if you must pay a $100 monthly service fee for the live-data feed, it is a worthwhile start-up cost. Most brokerage firms will have a fee similar to this or more; because you will not be executing real trades during this time, you will not be paying commissions to offset their costs. Despite the monthly cost, spending sufficient time doing simulation trading with live data will be an excellent and inexpensive way of learning. You need this risk-free trading experience prior to live trading. There is no substitute!

Some simulators use delayed data. You want live data so that you can learn and experience from all that happens in a live mode. With live simulated trading you will get to feel the influences of the news, trading-room activity, and the synergy of the market day. You will not get this experience with delayed data.

Some electronic brokerage companies will not let you open a trading account using the sophisticated trading software that you need unless you have already had experience as a trader. However, if you have had training as a trader or are currently participating in a training program, you should be able to open an account with a brokerage firm offering simulated trading with this state-of-the-art trading software. Call the brokerage firm to find out which training programs they consider sufficient to qualify you to open an account with them. This will take a telephone call or two, but it is definitely worth doing to ensure that you will be qualified to open an account.

Please see "Day-Trading Training Courses" earlier in this chapter for names and descriptions of some of these training programs. Be sure the training program uses the same software as the brokerage firm where you plan to open an account.

SureStart ⟩ *CyBerCorp's CyBerTrader Simulator*

CyBerCorp, without a doubt, has the best simulator available for simulation trading. We would consider it a two-step system for simulation trading. First, there is a free CyBerTrader simulator on the CyBerCorp Web site. This simulator uses the previous day's data for its data feed. For a free, unlimited-use simulator, you cannot beat this. You will experience CyBerTrader's software and get the feel for trading with Level II quotes in general. All the analytical tools available in the CyBerTrader software are available there. At the present time, you cannot receive the previous day's data on the S&P and Nasdaq futures.

Second, when you open and fund an account at CyBerBroker, you can do unlimited live simulation trading on CyBerTrader. All the functions and tools that are available for live trading are available in the simulator mode. There will be a fee for the service/live data feed during any period where you have fewer than 50 live executions. However, in our opinion, it is well worth using this system in order to benefit from the educational experience that simulated trading with live data brings to you. In addition, the CyBerTrader simulator allows for random fills. This adds to the reality of simulation trading since it behaves more like real trading where we often to do not get filled when we enter an order. Also in simulation trading in the live mode, you will have access to the S&P and Nasdaq futures, which is of great importance to part-time traders.

Please be advised that other brokerage companies using CyBer-Trader software may allow simulation trading with live data.

simulation trades

In simulation trading, enter each trade with the same diligence as you would if it were a live trade. Think in terms of placing your trade with your hard-earned dollars at risk. Be dead serious about each trade. Do not start simulation trading with the thought, "Oh, this is only practice. If I lose money, no big deal." Be forewarned: If you have that attitude in simulation trading, it will carry over into your live trading.

Trading Plan, Rules, and Discipline in Conjunction with
Simulated Trading

Prior to simulation trading, you must develop a trading plan, no matter how simple. Write the plan down so that you can follow it and if you go astray, you can see where. By writing the trading plan down, you may see opportunities for upgrading your plan while you are simulation trading. Incorporate these improvements into your plan. Also, before you practice trading, establish a set of rules that you are going to follow. Stick by your rules. Adherence to a good set of rules will keep you successful and will help you preserve your capital. At the top of your rules list, we suggest that you place the following: Keep my pre-set stop loss! You will find a whole section on stop losses later in this book.

Now that you have your trading plan and rules in place you will begin simulation trading. You can start implementing one of the most important facets of trading—discipline. We again stress that you consider every practice trade as important as any real trade. This way you can begin to see the strengths and weaknesses in your trading discipline and correct those weaknesses before you begin live trading. Without a trading plan and rules in place, you cannot develop your discipline, which is so vitally important to you as trader.

At this stage of simulation trading do not be concerned about whether your fill would have been executed in real life. That will be practiced after you get the basics down for trading strategies, rules, and discipline.

After you have selected one or two trading strategies and the appropriate analytical tools to use with these strategies, start off with a slow-moving, high-volume stock such as CSCO. Concentrate on just one or two stocks so you can start learning the patterns, the market makers' actions and the rhythm of the stock. It will take a while to get the feel of a stock, but once you have it, it will be extremely helpful to you in entering and exiting trades. With a slow-moving stock, you will have time to see and understand what is happening while you are in a trade. You will have time to learn and absorb what you see.

In a slow-moving stock you will see the action of the market makers moving between the bid and the ask and dropping or raising their price levels in relation to the price of the stock. You will be able to discern who the "Ax" is on a stock (the Ax is the key market maker of that stock on any particular day). More often than not, if you are watching the same stock, you might see the same market maker as the Ax on many days. In addition, with some software you will be able to see the Island book and/or see all the Island bids and asks integrated into the Level II stock box, which is a great way to watch the depth of stock at any given price level. This will help you gauge the direction of a stock's movement. If your software does not have access to all of the Island book data, you can go to their Web site on the Net, www.island.com, and view the full book live. With a slow-moving stock you will at least have a chance to see if your simulated execution and fill could have occurred as a live trade by viewing the TOS in the stock box.

If you start simulation trading on a fast-moving stock such as AMZN, all of the aforementioned benefits of watching a stock while in a trade go out the window. You would only be thinking about how to get out of your trade, and you would not have time to think of how to execute the exit most efficiently. Moreover, because the stock is moving so quickly, it could be very difficult to determine from the TOS whether you would have gotten a fill on a real trade.

When you have the fundamentals down cold on a slow-moving stock, then you can move up to a faster-moving stock. This will test your perception of a stock's activities in a shorter time period and with wider price fluctuations. After you try this a few times, you will see how difficult it is to watch what is happening in a fast-moving stock. Furthermore, it is almost impossible to enter and exit these trades with any certainty about what you are doing!

We suggest that you practice your trading with the same number of shares that you will be able to buy when you go live, but not to exceed 1,000 shares. Depending on the stock you trade, entering and exiting can be difficult to accomplish when you are buying more than 1,000 shares. Trading with more than 1,000 shares will require more advanced knowledge of order routing and execution than you will have in the early stages of your education. In reality, many well-known stocks would be difficult to enter and exit easily at 1,000 shares, particularly during the slow trading hours of the day when there is little volatility in a stock's price.

We suggest simulation trading using 100 to 200 shares, the same lot size of shares that we would recommend when you start trading live. This way, fills will more likely match what occurs in real time versus simulation trading. We also recommend, if your software allows, a random fill setting. With the random fill setting, you will not automatically get filled when you enter a buy or sell order. This lets you experience some of the anxieties that you will experience in real life when orders are not filled.

After you have traded live with 100 or 200 shares successfully and wish to move up in share size, do so first in simulation trading. Get successful in practicing the larger share lots. Then switch over to live trading of the same.

While trading in a simulation mode, we highly encourage you to keep a diary of your trading activities. Your comments do not have to be extensive, just meaningful. We advise you to jot your comments down immediately after a trade so that they will be accurate. At the end of the day, compare your comments about success or failure on each trade with your written trading plan and your rules. How do they match up? Where do you need improvements? What mistakes are repetitive? This is what simulation trading is all about: improving your skills, increasing your knowledge of trading strategies, and implementing your trading discipline.

Simulation trading lets you discover what type of trader you are, all at no risk to your trading capital! By testing your discipline and trading strategies, you will learn what is more suited to you as a part-time trader. Are you a scalper, a swing trader, or a short-term position trader?

The Real Value of Simulation Trading
What is the real value of simulation trading? Let's look at the answer to this from a broad perspective. While simulation trading, you are trying to enter trades in the direction of market movement. Even if you were filled on every order you entered, it is doubtful that you, as a beginning part-time trader, would have all trades continue in the direction you had expected. Even if every entry and movement in the next 30 seconds were in your favor, how many of you would get out with some profit? Not many. Why? Because inexperienced traders usually buy, see a small reversal, and do not even think about getting out of the trade. They stay in the trade until the trade has gone past their entry point, and they experience losses. So there will be losses in simulation trading.

In simulation trading, you will see if your trading strategies, rules, rhythm-recognition, and discipline are taking you in the right direction. Simulation trading is not about how much money you make. Forget that for now. In trading, you must first make good entries so that your trades flow in the direction anticipated, be it long or short. So, take careful note in your diary of your entries. Obviously, if you make money on the majority of your trades, you at least know you are doing something right. You made a profit because the stock had to move in your direction to get you that profit!

If you only made one-eighth of a point on every trade, and you notice that the stock you bought did not continue to go up, you would be building a weak case for your picking successful entry points. On the other hand, if you made three-eighths to one-half point on every trade, you could be feeling confident that your entries are getting good.

Getting into the trade is half the battle, so get that right first. Next, learn how to exit a trade. You already know what your stop loss is. It has been preset, so you know exactly how much you are willing to risk to determine if the stock is going in the direction of your trade. Depending on what type of trading style you are using, you will have a preset profit that you will take, particularly as a scalp trader. For some trading styles, you will set a trailing stop loss to protect your profits. This will definitely test your discipline. Let the simulator expose your weaknesses and then develop a plan to correct them. Regardless of how much you made or lost in your dummy account, check your notes: Are you taking your stop losses? Are you keeping your profits as planned by using a trailing stop loss? This is what simulation trading is all about.

Caution on Simulation Trading

Because of the ease of getting orders filled and the lack of real emotions that are only produced when your capital is at risk, you should be getting good at making dummy dollars, or "cyber dollars." This is good, of course! Just imagine if your weren't getting better. We would tell you to hang it up. However, do not let this success go to your head and do not allow yourself to think you are an experienced trader ready to make big money. We have another stage of simulated trading for you before you go live.

Tightening the Simulation Trade Executions

Now that you are successful in the basics, you can move up to another more definitive level of simulation trading where you pick entries and exits based on the reality of them being filled in live trading.

We now want you to consider picking a point of entry and execution that you think is likely to be filled in real-life trading. You can judge this by the action at the inside price levels, the amount of shares available, and the actual sales shown in TOS. Obviously, if a stock is moving up, you will probably not be filled on the bid, so do not use the bid as your price for entering the order. If the stock is moving up and there is only one market maker on the ask, don't use that price as your entry. Chances are, if you were trading live, you would not get filled at that price. If your software allows, buy at the next level up on the ask or wait for the one market maker on the inside ask to be taken out and buy on the new inside ask. Be realistic; think real life while doing simulated trading. If you go for a stock price that is unlikely to be filled in real-time trading, the only person you will be cheating is you.

Once you get filled on an order, look at the TOS. Were there enough sales to fill your order at the price you were filled by the simulator? If not, cross off that trade or add on one price level to the price where you placed your order. Use the same process when exiting. This will probably be a little more difficult to implement. If a trade goes against you when you are in a long position, it can drop sharply and everyone and his cousin will attempt an exit at the same moment. To be realistic, you have to pick a price several levels down on the bid as your exit point and wait for the price to get there and stabilize. To be fair to yourself, consider executing your sell at the stabilizing point re-gardless of how far down the price has dropped, as this is more likely to represent reality than any other exit price.

Determining whether a trade would have actually been executed will be based on each individual's assessment of what the TOS was do-ing at the time each trade was executed. You must be truthful to your-self in this process. If you are not, the assessment of whether you got filled or not will be useless, and any attempt at assessing how well you are doing in cyber dollars will have little meaning. Remember, too, that most software does not automatically calculate your profit and loss with commissions. So do not forget to deduct your commission expense from your profit and loss.

When to Simulation Trade
We suggest you use the same hours that will be available to you as a part-time trader for trading live. This way you will continue with the same feel and rhythm of the stocks when you begin live trading.

Presently, we do not recommend that the part-time trader begin their live trading during the premarket or after-market hours. We need to see more liquidity in these markets during these hours. It will not be long in coming and that will be good for all part-time traders.

After a three-day weekend, we will warm up for our live trading by beginning simulation mode with CyBerTrader. We will execute a few trades to make sure we are sharp using our keyboard, mouse, and execution routing. For the part-time trader, you can use the simulation mode of trading to keep your trading skills honed to perfection.

How Long Should Part-Time Traders Participate in Simulation Trading?
Never cut your simulation-trading time short: become very successful at it. As a part-time trader, expect this process to take three to six months or longer for short-term momentum trading; one to two months for the consolidation breakouts. The best case scenario for you would be to trade in simulation mode during three different market trends: up, down, and sideways. If you do your simulation trading through only one or two of these market trends, we suggest that you switch back to simulation trading when the market enters the trend you have not yet been through.

Continue simulated trading until you can consistently make dummy or cyber dollars at the level that you expect of yourself. When this is accomplished, you are ready to start trading with small share lots, live and with confidence!

Availability of Software for Simulation Trading
The following brokerage firm companies offer software for simulation trading for you to practice.

CyBerBroker, Inc.

CyBerTrader

Software: CyBerTrader

They offer unlimited, free on-line simulation trading using the previous day's data. Simulator is available at their Web site.

Unlimited live simulation trading is available after account is funded. Activate simulation trading by logging on in "DEMO" mode at www.cybercorp.com.

Other brokerage firms offer simulation trading using live data. However, the software, conditions, and length of time available to practice differ.

Since simulation trading is a significant part of your decision in selecting a particular brokerage firm, call these firms prior to funding an account to get a clear understanding of their present-day simulation trading policy.

chapter 5

SureStart trading strategies

Our **SureStart** recommendation consists of two trading strategies: short-term momentum trading and consolidation-breakout trading. Our consolidation-breakout strategy is for those who prefer a less fingernail-biting trading style as compared to short-term momentum trading. Successful implementation of these strategies is only possible after getting the right software, analytical tools, patience, discipline, and experience. However, experience is something that we cannot put into words for you. It will take time, perhaps three months to a year. You will see that these strategies work well for some part-time traders. Consolidation breakouts will be particularly attractive to traders with less trading capital and less tolerance for anxiety.

We furnish you an overview of the two different trading strategies. You can judge which strategy might work best for you in terms of your time allocation, capital, and money management. We do not expect that you will be able to master our strategies simply by reading through the material furnished in this book. Remember, the goal of this book is to point you in the right direction. Once you feel comfortable with a particular strategy, use the resources given at the end of our trading strategies to fully explore and learn all that is necessary to implement the strategy you have chosen.

There are obviously other trading strategies and technical indicators available to you. You will see these as you review our recommended resources, join an on-line trading room, and speak with other traders.

short-term momentum trading strategy

Short-term momentum trading is also known as scalping. A trade held for a short duration of time, usually 1 to 15 minutes, for a small profit of one-quarter point to a half point. This strategy is based on trading a stock off the stochastics reversal and bounce on one-minute charts. This will be explained in detail in this chapter. Your education as a part-time trader will come from watching and simulation trading of a stock that reverses with the stochastic reversals and bounces. We also use other indicators that will aid you in confirming the stochastic reversals. We will briefly explain these other indicators to you in this chapter so you will know what they are, but we do not expect you to know the theory behind each. We just want you to know how to use each. These other indicators will be Bollinger bands, moving averages, the one-minute and the five-minute candlestick chart, S&P futures and Nasdaq 100 futures, Nasdaq composite average, support and resistance levels. More detailed information on these indicators is given in this chapter. Additionally, please refer to our resource list at the end of this chapter. You can use a variety of indicator settings for all the technical analysis indicators. In addition to the settings suggested by us in this chapter, please refer to resources listed at the end of the chapter to help you choose the indicator settings, which would be most applicable to your trading style. Additionally, instructional courses will offer indicator settings with the trading strategies that they teach.

You will have to watch charts until you are blue in the face to gain experience in knowing the rhythm of the stocks you wish to trade in order to be successful with short-term momentum trading. You need to be able to see a true reversal forming with the stochastics and the signs of confirmation of that reversal. When we speak of the rhythm of a stock, we are speaking of the oscillations or wave patterns of a stock's price.

In trading, you will always hear people say, "The trend is your friend." This is very applicable to short-term momentum trading. The wisest advice we can give you is to go long stocks that are in an up-trend and to go short stocks that are in a downtrend. Always take a look at the daily chart to confirm that the stock is trending in the direction you are planning to trade. Trading is a business of putting the odds in your favor. You will have successful trades more often if you trade in the direction of the stock's daily trend.

the anatomy of the charts used in this book

All the charts that are used in this strategy are intraday charts. Charts have time intervals of one minute or five minutes. Please refer to the charts and descriptions that follow as a guide to some of the terms discussed in this section.

Candlestick charting is our preferred method for watching a stock's price movement. This method of charting and Figure 5.1 are described in the following section.

candlestick charting

Candlestick charting is our preferred method of watching a stock's price movement, as it is the most informative of all charting techniques.

The one-minute candlestick depicts a stock's opening price, closing price, high and low for the one-minute interval of a stock's price. In this book, the gray candle indicates an upward price movement from the opening of the time period. The closing price of the time period is higher than the opening price of the time period. The black candle indicates a downward price movement from the opening of the time period. The closing price of the time period is lower than the opening price of the time period.

As soon as you can afford to purchase Nison's two books on candlestick charting (at least his first), we would strongly recommend that you do so. The two books are listed in our Education Books section, in Chapter 4, Preparing to Trade.

---

figure 5.1 one-minute chart moving averages

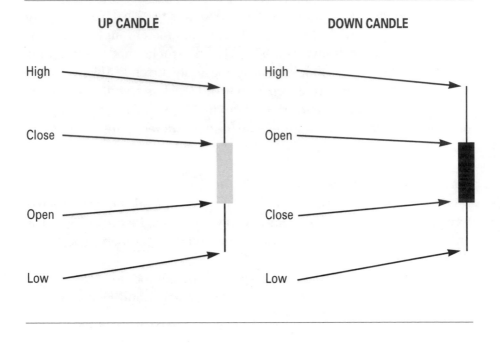

One-Minute Candlestick Price Movement (Upper chart section)
Figure 5.2

Gray candle: Upward price movement from the opening of the time period. The closing price of the time period is higher than the opening price of the time period.

Black candle: Downward price movement from the opening of the time period. The closing price of the time period is lower than the opening price of the time period. (Please refer to Figure 5.2.)

Moving averages (Upper chart section)

Black: Fast moving average

Gray: Slow moving average

figure 5.2 **one-minute intraday chart showing moving averages and stochastics**

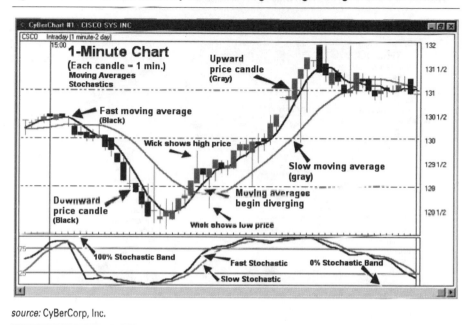

source: CyBerCorp, Inc.

Bollinger bands (Upper chart section) See Figure 5.3
Gray (2): (The upper most and lower most gray lines)

Stochastic bands (Lower chart section)
Black: Fast stochastic line
Gray: Slow stochastic line

what are stochastics?

Stochastics (stochastic indicator lines) compare the current price of a stock to its trading range over a given period of time in the past. It is an oscillator that shows short-term momentum of a stock within a trading range. This occurs between a low-price support level, where traders tend to buy, and a high-price resistance level where traders tend to sell.

figure 5.3   one-minute intraday chart showing Bollinger bands and volume

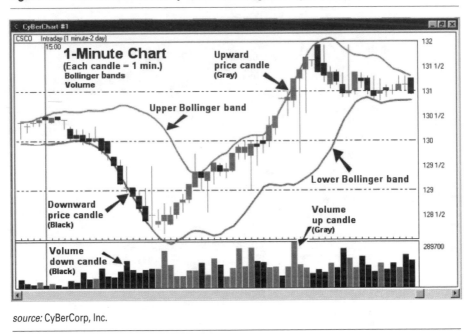

source: CyBerCorp, Inc.

There are two types of stochastics: a fast stochastic and a slow stochastic. The fast and slow stochastics are indicators that are each represented by a line in a separate graph below a stock's price chart. The stochastic reversals that we refer to here are the definitive turns of the stochastic lines that occur when the downward momentum in a stock's price reverses to an upward momentum, as in Figure 5.4. In this chart a buying opportunity exists in CSCO at approximately 3:23 P.M. (trade 2). Figure 5.4 also shows the opposite: a turn from upward to downward momentum in the stock's price. In this chart a shorting or short-sale opportunity exists in CSCO at approximately 3:04 P.M. (trade 1).

When we refer to a shorting or short-sale opportunity, we mean selling a stock you do not currently own. To go short, you borrow stock from your broker, then sell the stock, with the intent to buy the stock back at a lower price than you had initially sold it for.

figure 5.4   CSCO, 2-11-2000, one-minute chart

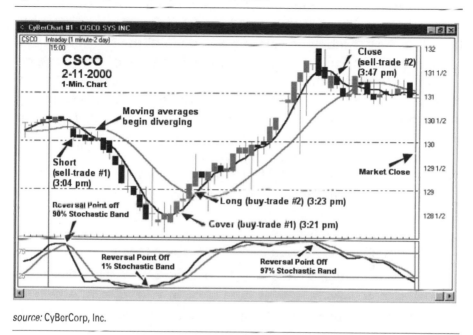

source: CyBerCorp, Inc.

The stochastic indicator is in a graph just below your price chart. Note that the stochastic bands run from zero at the bottom of the chart to 100 at the top. See Figure 5.2. You will also see that there are two stochastic lines that generally move parallel to each other. The black line is the fast-moving stochastic. The gray line, which is the moving average of the fast stochastic, is the slow-moving stochastic. We based our trading strategy on the movement of the fast-moving stochastic and use the slow-moving stochastic as a broader indication of a stock's price momentum. When stochastic lines rise, the price momentum is rising. When the lines are dropping, the opposite is true, the price momentum is falling.

The stochastic lines can appear to fall below the zero band or appear to go above the 100 band. However, these lines are just riding the zero or 100 band. As such, trading decisions are not made until the stochastic lines bounce off these bands and start moving in a reverse direction. After the fast stochastic line (black) reverses, we will usually wait until the fast-moving stochastic line cuts back through the slow-moving stochastic line (gray) before executing our trade. Additionally, we use caution on entering a trade until the fast-moving stochastic has cut back through the 15 percent band on a reversal upward and cut back through the 85 percent band on a reversal downward. Please see Figure 5.4. We will also wait to see other confirming indicators to be sure a reversal is of substance before acting on our trade. See "Using All Your Indicators" later in this chapter.

There can be different settings for stochastics. The settings that we use have two for the fast stochastic and three for the slow stochastic. Stochastic settings are usually entered under the following designations:

Fast Stochastic: Period 1 (__),   Period 2 (__)

Slow Stochastic: Period 1 (__),   Period 2, (__),   Period 3 (__)

We use the stochastic settings of 15 and 3 for the fast stochastic and 15, 5, and 2 for the slow stochastic.

Be sure to keep track of the colors that are associated with the fast and slow stochastic indicator lines.

Our description of stochastics and their settings is very simplistic. Please refer to the resource list at the end of this chapter for more descriptive and detailed information pertaining to stochastics.

what types of stochastic reversals are we looking for?

We are looking for those reversals that provide us with the highest percentage of winning trades. These are reversals from the stochastic zero to 10 bands or 100 to 90 bands, or very close to each, as shown in the various graphs in the chapter. Waiting for these situations to develop takes patience and discipline. However, they will occur, and usually do so, several times a day on any one stock. Additionally, a part-time trader could be watching several different stock charts, thus increasing the probability that a trading opportunity would present itself more frequently.

when do we look for the stochastic reversals?

Some market times are better than others for short-term momentum trading. The best times would be in the first three hours of trading and the last hour and a half of trading. Within these hours we pay particular attention around 9:50 A.M. to 10:05 A.M. EST for reversals and healthy bounces as the market makers usually have completed filling their orders by that time. Quite frequently the market will change direction in that time interval, long enough for some good trades. We also like the shorting possibilities from approximately 11:00 A.M. EST until 12:30 P.M. EST. However, be careful here as volume may have dried up and the lack of liquidity may make exiting a trade more difficult.

support and resistance levels

A resistance level is a price or value which an up trending stock or index has difficulty penetrating. A stock or index will often fall back in price or value after reaching the resistance level. Once a resistance line or level has been broken, it often becomes a support level. A support level is a price or value that a down trending stock or index has difficulty penetrating. Once the support line or level has been broken, it often becomes a resistance level.

When trading using stochastic indicators, we must keep a close eye on the support and resistance levels of S&P and Nasdaq futures, the Nasdaq 100 composite index, and the stock we wish to trade. This includes intraday and daily support and resistance levels. These are very important price or value levels, which can hold back a stock's upward or downward momentum. We recommend that you avoid entering any trade when a stock's price is near any major resistance or support levels, or if the S&P and Nasdaq futures or the Nasdaq 100 composite index are near major resistance or support levels. Wait to act on your stochastic indicators until you have seen these resistance or support levels broken.

We would highly recommend drawing the major support and resistance levels on your charts. This way you will not forget what those levels are when you are deeply engrossed in watching all the other indicators that we mention. New support and resistance levels are also formed during the day and these should be marked on your charts. Please refer to the next section of this chapter, entitled Consolidation-Breakout Strategy, for examples of support and resistance levels.

two moving averages help us confirm a reversal

A moving average may be the most widely used technical indicator in existence. It is a simple moving average of a stock's prices over a specific length of time. A continuous line on the stock price chart represents the moving average. We use two moving averages: a fast moving average, averaged over a short length of time; and a slow moving average, averaged over a longer length of time. We use a black line to represent the fast moving average and a gray line to represent the slow moving average. Please see "The Anatomy of Charts," Figure 5.2. When trading, our charts will show these two moving averages. Most traders use the moving average in order to determine the direction of a stock's trend.

We like to use simple moving averages to help us confirm a reversal in the stochastics of the stock we are watching. We first want to see that the fast-moving average begins to reverse its direction, then we want to see the slow-moving average also begins to reverse its direction to confirm a reversal. Finally, seeing the moving averages cross over is further confirmation that a reversal in the stochastics is legitimate. The more the fast-moving average diverges or separates from the slow-moving average and the sharper the angle, the more solid the confirmation of a stochastic reversal. See Figures 5.2 and 5.4 for examples of this. Moving averages for momentum trading vary; our one-minute graphs show moving averages of five periods for the fast and ten periods for the slow. Another widely used set of settings is ten and twenty for five-minute graphs. Moving average settings are usually entered under the following designations:

(Fast) moving average: Period (____)

(Slow) moving average: Period (____)

Note: Your setting indications in your software will usually state "moving averages" or "MA" with the period designation. After setting the period designation for one MA, set the other MA at a different period. Hence, the two MAs. Be sure you know what color or style represents each MA.

Bollinger bands help us spot a reversal

Bollinger bands are continuous bands that vary in distance from a moving average based on volatility. The upper band is sometimes referred to as the "upper channel line" and represents x number of standard deviations above the average, based on volatility. The lower band is sometimes referred to as the lower channel line and represents x number of standard deviations below the average. The space between the two lines is known as the *channel*. The bands are self-adjusting for volatility in a stock's price, widening during volatile price action and contracting during tighter trading ranges. Sharp price action can be expected to follow a tightening of the bands. We emphasize that this price action can be in either direction: up or down.

Two lines overlaid on the stock price chart represent Bollinger bands. We use gray for both the upper and lower bands. Please refer to "The Anatomy of Charts" section and Figure 5.3. In actual practice we have Bollinger bands; stochastic indicators, moving averages; and volume on the same graph. (This is possible through the use of different colors for each indicator on your computer screen.)

The closer a stock's price moves to the upper Bollinger band, the more overbought the stock is. In this situation a condition exists in which a stock's price has recently experienced a sharp rise in price and is vulnerable to a price drop because there are fewer buyers left to drive the price up any further.

The closer a stock's price moves to the lower Bollinger band, the more oversold the stock is. In this situation a condition exists in which a stock's price has recently experienced a sharp drop in price and may be due for a rise in price because there are few sellers left in.

We like to use Bollinger bands to help us decide when the start of a reversal in the stochastic could be most favorable for us. In going long on a reversal from the zero stochastic band, we like the first upward one-minute candles to originate from the bottom channel line of the Bollinger band or slightly below. For going short on a reversal from the 100 stochastic bands, we want to see the first downward one-minute candles originate from the upper channel line of the Bollinger band or slightly above. This gives us more room to move within the Bollinger band channel. More often than not, we pick up our scalping profit within the channel lines. Notice the position of the candles relative to the Bollinger bands as the price starts to climb in Figure 5.3. The upward-price candles move way from the bottom of the Bollinger bands. Not coincidentally, this occurs at the same time the stochastics are reversing from the zero stochastic band, as seen in Figure 5.2.

Additionally, note in Figure 5.3 how the price candles move away from the top of the Bollinger bands as the price starts to drop. Again, this is occurring from the reversal of the stochastic at the 100 percent band as shown in Figure 5.2.

As the trading range of the stocks becomes smaller, the Bollinger bands also become tighter, as shown in the upper-right-hand corner of Figure 5.3. A tight trading range of a stock's price indicates a consolidation period and is the basis of our other trading strategy, consolidation breakouts.

When the candlesticks appear above or below the channel formed by the Bollinger bands, we must exercise caution in entering trades on reversals as the stock may be continuing the present trend. It would be wise to wait before taking action on a trade, based on a stochastic reversal, until you see the candlesticks come back within the range of the Bollinger bands. Please refer to Figure 5.4 and the 11:56 and 11:57 candles at the reversal from above the Bollinger band of YHOO and the 12:31 candle at reversal from below the Bollinger band of YHOO in Figure 5.5.

Bollinger band settings are varied in choice. We use period settings of 13, 2.62, and 2.62. Settings of 9, 2, and 2 can also be used.

Settings will usually be designated as the following:

Bollinger bands: Period 1 (_____)

Period 2 (_____)

Period 3 (_____)

other stochastic bounces solidify the stochastic reversal in the stock we are watching

When looking for trading opportunities, especially in the Nasdaq 100 stocks, we are always watching the S&P and Nasdaq 100 futures and the one-minute stochastics for each. These two futures indices are reflective of what buyers and sellers are willing to pay for stocks contained in the indices as an aggregate at an agreed upon price at a certain time in the future. As such, the futures indices are considered lead indicators of the future movement of the price of stocks contained

figure 5.5   YHOO, 2-14-2000, with Bollinger bands and volume

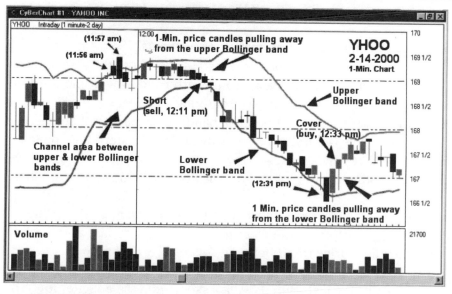

source: CyBerCorp, Inc.

in these indices. Let us say, cautiously, that the futures are predictive of the price of these stocks as a whole.

When we see that the futures indices have made a stochastic reversal near the zero band with a bounce to the upside, we will pay particular attention to our stocks to see if stochastic reversals are beginning to form there, too. The futures reversal and bounce, depending on the intensity, can foreshadow similar reversals and bounces in the stocks that we are watching. By seeing the futures reverse and rise, we feel more comfortable in going long on a stock. The reverse is true for shorting.

These similar patterns of stochastic reversals in the futures and in the stocks we are watching obviously do not occur all the time. However, when they do occur together, we want to be ready. If we are ready to go long in a stock and the futures rise and the stochastics reverse from a support level, it is a confirmation of the reversal we see taking place in the stock we wish to trade, or in this case, to buy. This, coupled with other indicators being positive, could make for a good entry point on your buy. The opposite of this would be true for going short. For an excellent example of the futures helping you in a trade, see Figures 5.8 and 5.9 in the section, "Using All Your Indicators," later in this chapter.

one-minute candles and confirmation of a reversal

Once a stochastic reversal has been established from the zero stochastic band, we like to see at least two upward candles with the third upward candle starting to build before entering a trade long. See Figure 5.4. After a reversal off the 100 percent band, we would want to see two downward candles with the third downward candle starting to build before going short. See Figure 5.4. However, nothing is cast in concrete. Depending on other confirmations, you may enter a trade sooner or later.

a higher low, the last gasp down . . . a confirmation of a reversal up

A befitting description, the "last gasp" is a stock's last and final attempt to hold a price trend before it reverses. So before we use words to explain this, look at Figure 5.6 to see an example of a last gasp down. Usually, the last gasp down is associated with a higher low. The higher-low candle is established when the low price of a stock reaches a trough that is higher than the previous low trough. Watching for higher lows in stocks and indices is a good way of determining the beginning of uptrends.

In Figure 5.6, CSCO shows CSCO after a downtrend and a reversal to the upside. At 2:59 P.M., CSCO begins a long downtrend making a low of 126⅝ at 3:09 P.M. From 3:10 P.M. to 3:13 P.M. the stock trades up to 127¼. CSCO then drops again to a higher low of 126¾ at 3:15 P.M. This is the last gasp candle down. Then the candle at 3:16 P.M. goes higher, as do subsequent candles, and the stochastics reversal to the upside continues.

In a reversal such as this, we would like to see one or two downward candles formed as an attempt to fight off the beginning of an upward price movement as in the 3:13 P.M., 3:14 P.M., and 3:15 P.M. candles. Next we like to see the formation of a strong upward candle as the 3:16 P.M. candle in the direction of the reversal after the higher low or last gasp downward candle at 3:15 P.M.

This is a good confirmation for the stochastic reversal we see beginning. After watching for a few more indicators to confirm an entry long on this trade, including the MA crossover at 3:18 P.M., we would enter this trade midway of the 3:18 P.M. candle or around 127⅛.

We would definitely exit this trade during the formation of the down candle beginning at 3:34 P.M. Just as the stochastics aid you in getting in a trade, they aid you in getting out. You will note that by 3:34 P.M. the stochastics have reversed from the 93 percent band and are heading downward.

It is quite likely that during the formation of the 3:23 P.M. downward candle that we may have exited with one half of our share purchases and held the balance until 3:34 P.M. If we have doubt of a trade continuation in the direction of the reversal, it is best to take some profits and let the rest ride. In this case, we would have definitely let the unsold balance of our shares or even the total amount ride as the MAs, as well as other indicators, were trending strongly upward. However, please remember it is never wrong to take profits, full or partial. If you had taken partial profits on half of your shares, at the first downward candle you would have made one-half point. If you held the balance until the first major indicators of a reversal downward, you would have made a one-point gain.

figure 5.6   CSCO, 2-16-2000, 1-minute chart showing moving averages and stochastics

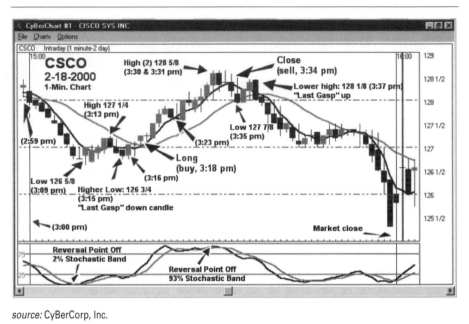

source: CyBerCorp, Inc.

a lower high, the last gasp up . . . a confirmation of a reversal down

Figure 5.7, YHOO, shows us a stock's last and final attempt to hold a price trend up before it reverses. Thus, an example of the last gasp up. Usually, the last gasp up is associated with a lower high. The lower high candle is established when the high of a stock's price reaches a peak that is lower than the previous peak. Watching for lower highs in stocks and indices is a good way of determining the beginning of downtrends.

Figure 5.7, YHOO, shows a downtrend beginning with the high candle of $167^{7}/_{16}$ at 11:57 A.M. After several downward candles we have several upward candles to another high candle of $167^{7}/_{16}$ at 12:02 P.M. Then we have several downward candles from the high candle of $167^{7}/_{16}$ and then a few candles back up to what is a lower high candle of $169^{3}/_{8}$ at

12:06 P.M. This is our last gasp up candle. After this candle our stochastic reversal continues downward with more downward candles.

What we like to see for confirmation of a reversal is one or two upward candles formed as an attempt to fight off the beginning of a downward price movement as in the 12:05 P.M. and 12:06 P.M. price candles, with the 12:06 P.M. price candle being the lower-high candle. Next we would like to see the formation of a comparatively large candlestick in the direction of reversal, or downward, as in the 12:07 P.M candle. We see this as a good confirmation for the stochastic reversal. It is time to consider entering a short trade. However, we do not enter yet as we will wait for other confirmations of a reversal utilizing our other indicators. Based on other indicators we enter a short trade at 12:11 P.M. In "Using All Your Indicators," we show you all the graphs associated with the other indicators that helped establish an entry point on this YHOO trade.

Please observe Figure 5.7 again. A high of 169^7/$_{16}$ forms at 11:57 A.M., then a price drop of several candles along with a drop in the stochastics to approximately the 70 percent band. If one were to use the stochastics and price candles on this chart alone, an entry might have been made at 11:58 A.M. or 11:19 A.M., but the moving averages would have told you to hold off a little longer.

After entering this trade at 12:11 P.M., we would exit this trade at 12:33 P.M. after seeing two strong candles moving up from a low at 12:31 P.M. Additionally, just as the stochastics help you get in, they tell you when to get out. As you can see in the chart, Figure 5.7, the stochastics have bounced and reversed from the 4 percent band. We would have made a good gain, approximately two points.

Later in the this section we will discuss exiting strategies. However, let us point out on this trade that we probably would have covered half our shares during the time period of 12:15 P.M. to 12:18 P.M. We would have let the balance of our shares ride to the 12:33 P.M. exit time.

For a good example of a lower high or last gasp up, see Figure 5.6, CSCO. A high is formed at 3:31 P.M., a low at 3:35 P.M., and a lower high at 3:37 P.M. In viewing all indicators on this chart alone, a good entry for a short would have been on the next downward candle, 3:38 P.M., if we could get in.

the five-minute chart confirmation

We watch only one Level II window on our screen at a time. We do this to avoid confusion and to be more focused on the stock that we expect to be trading. We highly suggest this to you new part-time traders as well. For the stock that we are watching in our Level II window, we have a one-minute intraday chart and a five-minute intraday chart tied to that Level II window. When we type in a new stock name in the stock box, the two charts for that stock automatically appear. In watching for reversals in the one-minute charts, we want to be sure that the reversals are real and that we will get a healthy bounce for a profit of at least a one-quarter or one-half point. This is where the five-minute chart helps. If you see your five-minute price chart trending steadily in one direction, be wary about trading any one-minute stochastic reversal against that trend until you see some indication of a change of trend in the five-minute price chart. The curvature of the fast MA on the five-minute price chart will be your first indication of trend reversal. Also, look for the five-minute stochastics to be reversing and bouncing. Figure 5.10 shows examples of both. You can find Figure 5.10 in the section titled, "Using All Your Indicators."

When you are looking at a the one-minute chart, you are looking at detail and sometimes not seeing the big picture. This is where the five-minute chart can help you in your decision to enter a one-minute stochastic reversal trade. It lets you see the big picture of a stock's trend. We usually draw our support, resistance and trend lines on the five-minute charts. Examples of these lines are given in the following section entitled "Consolidation-Breakout Strategy."

are we asking for too much confirmation of a reversal?

We think not. The number of times that all these confirmations come into play on a high-volume stock is amazing. Two, three, or four times a day is not unusual. We know realistically that not all these confirmations will appear and be textbook perfect, nor will they all be present at the same time. This is where experience comes into play. Watch charts of just a few stocks to start (two to four charts are suggested) to see these stochastic reversals forming. Watch closely for the confirmations to develop. After you start feeling that you can identify a high percentage of the reversals with bounces sufficient enough to earn a profit, start executing some simulation trades. Then move up to live trading, trading small share lots. Remember that the key is patience and discipline in waiting for the right moment to enter your trade. Like a lioness, wait for the right opportunity to attack your prey!

using all your indicators

Below are four charts that were being watched while trading YHOO on February 14, 2000. By assessing the data from all four charts, an entry point for a short was found as was an exit point. By watching all the charts shown in Figures 5.7 to 5.10, one could stay in this trade a little longer than usual and do a little better than the usual one-quarter to one-half point scalp. In Figure 5.7, YHOO could have been shorted just after breaking through the 169 support level and then covered at $168^{1}/_{8}$. Alternately you could have covered half your shares at $168^{1}/_{8}$ and covered the balance at $167^{1}/_{8}$. A more conservative time to short would have been during the 1:13 P.M. candle after the S&P and Nasdaq futures broke below their support levels. See Figures 5.8 and 5.9. With experience you will be able to judge when you should enter and exit trades and which indicators are most important to follow with your style of trading. Notice that all the indicators in the YHOO five-minute chart, Figure 5.10, generally continued in a downtrend from 11:10 A.M. to 2:00 P.M. Please note there are no Bollinger bands in the Nasdaq and S&P futures charts, Figures 5.9 and 5.10. Bollinger bands would normally be on both futures charts. However, to simplify these charts, they were not included in this book.

we got you in, now we have to get you out

You have successfully entered your trades. You are statistically successful 70 percent of the time in getting a bounce after a reversal where you had the opportunity to lock in at least one-half point gain. Capture your profits or take some of your profits and possibly let some profits ride. It is psychologically very important that you lock in profits. If you go beyond one-half point and do not take profits or take only partial profits, you must initiate a mental preset trailing stop loss for going forward. Remember do not be greedy. Get out when you can,

figure 5.7   YHOO, 2-14-2000, one-minute chart

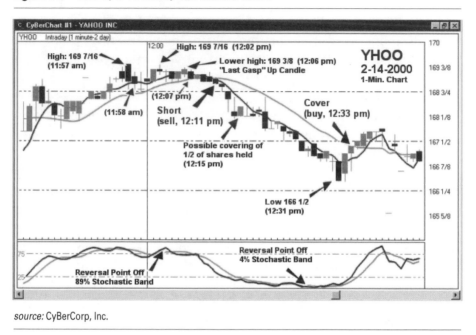

source: CyBerCorp, Inc.

not when you have to. (Please refer to the section, "The Importance of Stop Losses" in this book.)

If you are still in your position, or in a partial position, with the trade moving in your favor, watch all your indicators to see if they are still looking good, particularly your five-minute chart (the big picture). When your indicators are warning you of a change, it's time to get out. If you are still in the trade and your trailing stop loss is coming up, act and get out. There is no second-guessing here if you wish to be successful as a part-time trader.

If you are in a trade (in this example, long), and you see a major downward candle formed on the one-minute S&P futures, get out of your trade immediately! S&P futures are predictive in nature, and the major downward candle is telling you the markets may be reversing. No need to wait for any confirmations here. If the signal turns out to be false, you can always get back in. However, if the signal is valid and

figure 5.8 S&P futures, 2-14-2000, one-minute chart

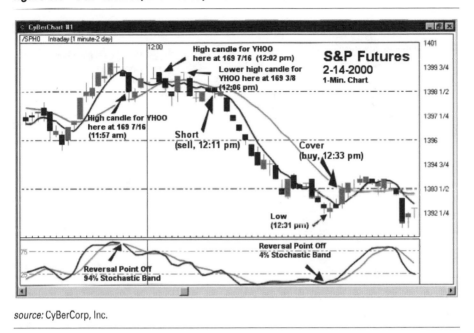

source: CyBerCorp, Inc.

you don't act immediately, you may be waiting in line to exit your trade with all the other traders trying to get out as the markets drop. This is a major warning of a possible downturn in the market. Be safe and get out when you can, not when you have to!

On the other 30 percent of your trades that have turned against you, there is only one answer: Take your preset stop loss without hesitation, thought, or reasoning. As Nike, says, "Just Do It!" By taking your stop loss here, you will protect those profits that you earned in the other 70 percent of your trades.

a summary for part-time traders

Normally, you should not execute a trade immediately after a stochastic reversal point. The stochastic reversal point and initial bounce starts the decision process on entering a trade. The actual entry is based on the presence of additional indicators confirming that a

figure 5.9   Nasdaq 100 futures, 2-14-2000, one-minute chart

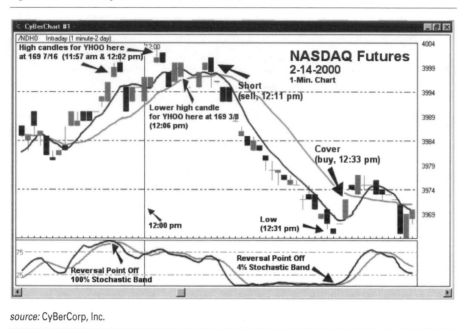

source: CyBerCorp, Inc.

reversal is significant enough to warrant entering the trade. These confirming indicators may appear quickly or come several minutes or longer after the stochastic reversal has occurred. This is where your experience in watching reversals and other confirming indicators will help you develop the appropriate entry points on your trades.

Always remember where the support and resistance levels are for the stock you are trading, the S&P and Nasdaq futures, and the Nasdaq composite index. You need to make sure there is room between the support and resistance levels and your entry point to earn a respectable profit. Ask yourself, "If the upward momentum stopped when my stock hits its next resistance, would I be able to make a profit?"

Additionally, once you decide to enter a trade, many other traders may have made the same decision. Your order may not be filled, or you may only receive a partial fill. If your order is not filled at

figure 5.10 YHOO, 2-14-2000, five-minute chart

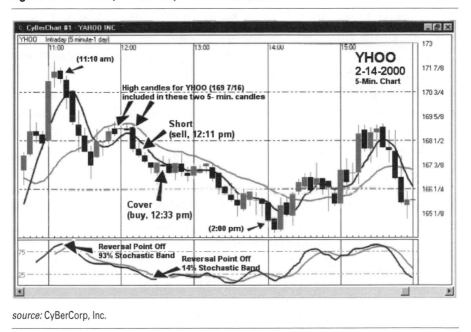

source: CyBerCorp, Inc.

the price you want, think carefully before placing an order at a different price. Frequently it is better to wait patiently for the next reversal. There is always the next trade. Practicing this restraint has proven successful for us.

If your order is partially filled, it is often best to cancel the rest of the order. Depending on the size of the fill and the stock's momentum, this is usually a safer approach. Why? Immediately after you get filled, you need to prepare for your exit in case the stock's price goes against you. If you are concentrating on filling the balance of your order, you might miss the opportunity to exit at a small loss should the stock's price reverse. Better to be safe than sorry.

We have given you a simple trading strategy used by many traders as their bread and butter trading technique. Nothing fancy, just something that works if you have patience, discipline, and take stop losses automatically.

consolidation-breakout trading strategy

We searched high and low for a technique that was low risk, low adrenaline, and yet high in potential for gain. We want to trade, not gamble. We want to make money, not place bets. Because of our need to develop a method to generate consistent income without the emotional highs and lows that come from pure momentum trading, we are bringing you an approach that is calm, steady, based on technical analysis, and good for part-time traders. And we will direct you to a superior chat room for identifying stocks that are great for consolidation breakouts.

The underlying theory here is that stock prices don't go straight up or straight down. An up-trending stock will go up, then level out for a while, then resume its move upward. Similarly, a down-trending stock will have prices that drop for a while, then level off, then resume their move downward. The period of time during which the price movement has leveled off or flattened is called a consolidation.

This pattern of a stock rising, consolidating, and then resuming its upward movement can be seen on daily charts and on intraday charts. As short-term traders, we are particularly interested in identifying these patterns on intraday charts. Our favorites are the one-minute and the five-minute intraday charts. We will first describe some consolidation patterns, and then we will discuss how to trade these patterns to take advantage of breakouts.

what is an intraday consolidation?

Let's start with a picture that will show an intraday consolidation pattern. On January 20, 2000, Healtheon Corp (HLTH) was experiencing upward momentum. On January 19, it closed at $44\frac{1}{2}$, and opened on January 20 at $44\frac{15}{16}$. Momentum came into the stock immediately, and by 11:00 A.M., it had risen to $47\frac{11}{16}$—a point gain of $2\frac{3}{4}$. See the graph of five-minute data on HLTH shown on Figure 5.11.

In general, when a stock has had a major percentage advance in such a short time, it will enter a period of consolidation. This consolidation is a period of time during which the stock moves sideways in a narrow range. In a way, this can be thought of as the pause that re-

figure 5.11   HLTH 1-20-2000, five-minute chart with two consolidations

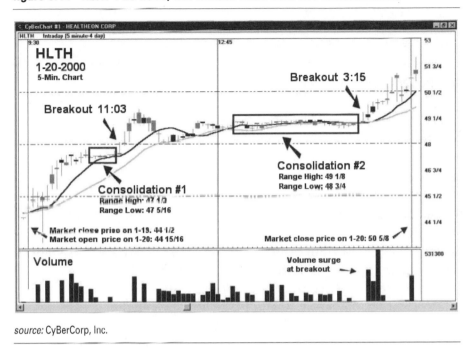

source: CyBerCorp, Inc.

freshes. The stock is resting at a new high for the day. If the owners of the stock felt that this was as high as the stock was going to rise on the day, they would start to book their profits by selling the stock. If enough owners had this belief, the stock would start to pull back as sellers came into the market and started to outnumber buyers. But if you observe that a consolidation is taking place, then the data is telling you that the number of sellers is not outnumbering the new buyers. On balance, the consensus of current owners is that the stock is likely to go up in price. The current owners are not selling and booking profits now because they believe that the stock is likely to move up further. They believe that holding onto the stock a little longer will maximize their profits.

This process of consolidation, which is reflected in the sideways pattern of price movement, is visually displaying this balance of current owners, buyers, and sellers. New buyers are coming into the market in sufficient quantity to satisfy the demand for the minority of current owners who want to sell at this point. Over the time the consolidation continues, the sellers become exhausted. When no other sellers come forward at this price, the price starts to move up again to accommodate new buyers, and the upward trend resumes.

At 1:00 P.M. this upward movement again pauses and the stock consolidates again. An even number of buyers and sellers again control the stock. This consolidation lasts for a little over two hours with no dips occurring in the price. At 3:15 P.M. the upward movement resumes and continues until the market closes.

to understand consolidations, you first need to understand support and resistance

An extremely important concept is that of support and resistance. This concept applies in both daily and intraday time periods. Let's first consider a stock that has recently moved upward. As the price of a stock moves up, it will hit certain prices that it can't penetrate immediately. At those prices, the stock will reverse and go through a mild pull back, or retracement to lower prices. If the stock is in a strong trend up, it will resume its upward movement until it again reaches a price that it can't immediately penetrate. These prices are points of resistance. The stock resists penetration, goes through a slight retracement, and then moves upward until it reaches its next point of resistance. See the daily graph of PTVL shown on Figure 5.12.

PTVL hit resistance 1, and then suffered a slight retracement before it continued its move up to resistance 2, where it went through another retracement. It then moved further up until it hit resistance 3. In this case, resistance 3 was the end of the uptrend and the beginning of a downtrend in this stock.

As a stock moves down from its high, you will see that the old resistance points now become points of support. As the price falls, the fall will be slowed or halted at or near most of the price points that formerly served as resistance. These former resistances now become supports. In Figure 5.12 you can see that as the price of PTVL started

figure 5.12   PTVL daily graph illustrating daily support and resistance

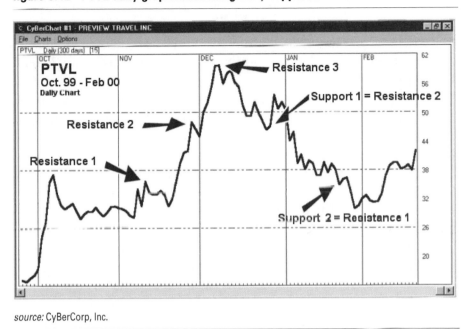

source: CyBerCorp, Inc.

going down after it hit resistance 3, the earlier resistance areas became the new support areas.

Things will not always be this perfect, but the following will usually occur:

Price increases will slow or halt at points of resistance.

Price decreases will slow or halt at points of support.

Prices that serve as resistance when the stock price is rising will serve as support as the stock reverses in price.

Prices that serve as support when the stock price is falling will become resistance when the stock starts to move back up.

This concept applies on both a daily basis and on an intraday basis. Before trading any stock, you should identify its intraday support and resistance levels. If you are considering buying a stock (going long) at a price of 40, you must know whether the next point of resistance is at $40\frac{1}{2}$ or at 50. The success of your trades depends on the likelihood that the stock will continue to move up, and that likelihood is greatly enhanced if the next point of resistance is not immediately above your entry point.

In addition to knowing the intraday points for price support and resistance, you must also know what prices serve as price support and resistance on a daily basis. The daily price supports and resistances will also act as price support and resistance intraday. So, if a stock has a daily high of $40\frac{1}{2}$, then you can expect that stock to slow or halt its upward momentum intraday when it approaches the price of $40\frac{1}{2}$. The daily price resistance of $40\frac{1}{2}$ has become an intraday resistance.

Price support and resistance are determined visually by analyzing the daily chart and the intraday five-minute chart. When you are considering trading any stock, look at these charts and write down all prices that may act as support and resistance. These support and resistance levels must always be part of your consideration when trading a stock.

We have gone through this discussion of price support and resistance because it is critical for trading using the consolidation-breakout strategy. We will show you how support and resistance are determined in consolidations and how they define your entry points for your trade and your stops for exiting the trade.

Properties of Consolidations
In consolidations, the trend is your friend. When prices are moving sideways in a narrow range, the thing you know with certainty is that the prices will eventually break out of that range. They will start moving either higher or lower. If the market is strong, or at least not in a strong selling mode, then consolidations that have occurred after strong upward movement intraday will tend to move or break in the direction of the trend prior to the consolidation, which in the case of HLTH on January 20 was upward. Similarly, if a consolidation occurs in a

stock that has experienced a strong downward movement intra-day, the prices will more likely break the consolidation by moving downward.

In consolidations, the longer the sideways movement has continued, the stronger the potential upward or downward movement when the stock breaks out of its consolidation range. On the January 20 HLTH chart (Figure 5.11), the stock broke out of consolidation 2 at 3:15 P.M. from a range high of $49^1/_8$. Between 3:15 P.M. and 4:00 P.M. when the market closed, HLTH rose to $50^5/_8$. The next morning it opened at $51^1/_8$. By the close of January 21, HLTH had zoomed up to $59^9/_{16}$. The long afternoon consolidation on January 20 gave us a clue about the potential for this substantial point gain. Remember that the longer the consolidation continues, the greater the potential for upward (or downward) movement when the consolidation ends.

In consolidations, the bottom of the range serves as price support and the top serves as resistance. This clearly defines a price for entering the trade and one for setting your stop. When the price breaks above the upper range, it has broken through a strong resistance and is ready to move up again with gusto! This is a sign that resistance has been broken and this breakout will be part of your entry strategy for getting into the trade. The best part is this: You also know that the bottom of the consolidation range is now acting as price support, and if you decide to go long in an up-trending stock, you have a natural place to set your stop. It is set immediately below the lower range of the consolidation. If the stock falls *below* that lower price range, then it has broken below its support, and the likelihood that it will fall further is greatly increased. So anytime you are long and the stock has broken below its major support, you want to sell your position. If you are going long, set your stop loss immediately below the lowest price in the consolidation range. If you are going short, set your stop loss immediately above the highest price in the consolidation range. Exit as soon as the stock trades at your stop price.

so what's the stock strategy, already?

You now know that stocks in a strong upward trend tend to keep moving up unless market forces are very negative, strangling this upward movement. You know that consolidations are resting periods where strongly up-trending stocks trade sideways for a while until their upward movement resumes. And you know that the tight range of the consolidation is defining a strong support price and a strong resistance price. Now let's convert this knowledge into a safe trading strategy. For simplicity, I will talk about uptrending stocks where we intend to take a *long* position, i.e., we intend to buy the stock. If you intend to short a downtrending stock, everything applies in reverse.

First, look for a strongly up-trending stock intraday. This could take place in three ways:

1. The stock may have gapped up at the open (opened higher than previous day's close) and then gone up further since the open.

2. The stock may have opened near the prior day's close and then run up sharply during the day.

3. The stock may have gapped up from the previous day's close and then consolidated at the opening price, which was sharply higher than the previous day's close.

The key criterion is that the stock has gone up very recently and is now trading sideways at the high of the day or very near the high of the day. The buy signal occurs when the stock price breaks through the high of the consolidating range. We prefer to look at the intraday stock prices on a five-minute candlestick chart. As you can see in Figure 5.13, MAXY has been consolidating in a range from 116 to 119. At 3:00 P.M., the stock breaks above the high of that consolidation range. The point at which the price breaks through the high of the range is now the signal to buy this stock.

The logic for this buy signal is simple. The bottom of the consolidation acts as support and the top acts as resistance. During the time of the consolidation, the stock is resting. When the stock begins to

figure 5.13 MAXY five-minute chart illustrating buy signal

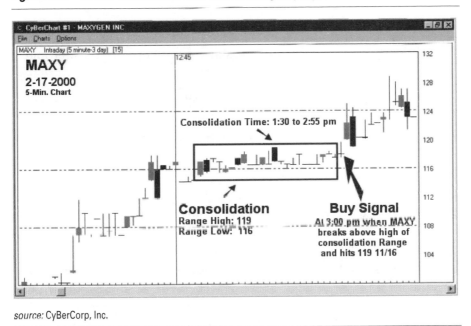

source: CyBerCorp, Inc.

trade above the top of its consolidation, it has broken through resistance and is ready to resume its upward price movement.

what can go wrong and how can you protect yourself from bad trades?
We will take our simple strategy and add ingredients, called risk reducers, to refine our trading strategy. Each ingredient you add reduces your trading risk. The more risk reducers you add, the better your trades will be. With practice, you will be able to add all these risk reducers to each trade you make. These are the seven risk reducers we favor:

Risk Reducer (RR)	*Procedure to Reduce Risk*
RR 1.	Long consolidations are best
RR 2.	Price must break above the consolidation range

RR 3.	Price break should occur with increased volume
RR 4.	S&P futures, Nasdaq 100 futures aligned
RR 5.	Intraday resistance or support allows room for successful trade
RR 6.	Daily resistance or support allows room for successful trade
RR 7.	Daily trend is in alignment with your trade

RR 1. Long Consolidations Are Best
Choose stocks that have consolidated for at least 15 minutes in the morning or for at least 30 minutes in the afternoon (EST).

RR 2. Price Must Break Above the Consolidation Range
Wait until the stock trades at least one-eighth above the high of the consolidation range. In Figure 5.12, HLTH consolidation 2 had a range of $48^3/_4$ to $49^1/_8$. The buy signal occurred after HLTH traded at $49^1/_4$. Increase this amount proportionally as the price of the chosen stock is increased. This amount is approximately equal to the maximum spread between the inside bid and the inside ask. Notice that this spread varies over time, so look for the largest spread you see during times of volatility.

RR 3. Price Break Should Occur with Increased Volume
Check the trading volume on your charts at the time of the break. If the break is going to be successful, it will come with increasing volume. If the volume increases as the price rises above the consolidation range, you are far more likely to have the price continue to move up. If the volume does not increase, a retracement back into the consolidation range could occur.

RR 4. S&P Futures, Nasdaq 100 Futures Aligned
Always keep an eye on the S&P and Nasdaq 100 futures. They serve as early warning devices when conditions arise that may produce sudden changes in the market. In particular, immediately before program

selling occurs, you will see the futures start to shoot downward. We always have one-minute charts of the S&P Futures and the Nasdaq 100 futures on our computer screen. By keeping the two futures charts in clear view and checking each before entering a position long (or short), you get confirmation that you are entering the trade in alignment with the current market trend. This should significantly reduce the number of times you will get shaken out of the trade almost immediately after entering it because of a sudden market turnaround.

RR 5. Intraday Resistance or Support Allows Room for Successful Trade
Before entering long, be sure you know how much room the stock has for going up before it encounters resistance. Resistance can be from a previous intraday high. This would occur if the stock ran to its intraday high and then fell back a little and consolidated. When the stock breaks this consolidation, it will encounter resistance at that previous intraday high. So you need to be sure that there is enough room between the high of the consolidation and the previous high. Similarly, if you are going to short a stock at the consolidation and the consolidation is above the day's low, that intraday low will be a support point and may halt or slow the fall of the stock. Be sure there is sufficient room between your entry and the day's low to allow for a reasonable profit in case the downward movement stops at that support.

RR 6. Daily Resistance or Support Allows Room for Successful Trade
Always look at a daily chart to determine the daily support and resistance. If a stock has consolidated at its intraday high and then breaks, it will encounter resistance at any areas of resistance on the daily chart. Be sure there is sufficient distance between your entry and the next level of resistance on the daily chart if going long, or between your entry and the next level of support on the daily chart if going short.

RR 7. Daily Trend Is in Alignment with Your Trade
As we've said before, "The trend is your friend," so go long on uptrending stock and go short on down-trending stocks. Always take a

quick look at the daily chart to confirm that the stock is moving in the direction you are planning to trade. Can a down-trending stock break above a consolidation? Yes, it can happen, but trading is a business of putting the odds in your favor, and you will have successful trades more often if you trade in the direction of the stock's daily trend. See Figure 5.14. CSCO is in an obvious uptrend. Before you enter a consolidation breakout on the long side, make sure that the stock you are entering is also in an uptrend.

This list of seven risk reducers is extremely important. At first it seems like a lot to be looking at, but with practice, it becomes very natural to enter a trade only after using all these risk reducers. In order to use all these risk reducers, we have arranged our computer screen to link together most charts needed for trading consolidations. The screen that we look at has the following five items on it at all times:

figure 5.14   daily graph of CSCO illustrating strong up-trending stock

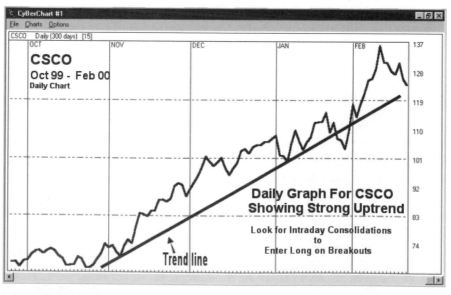

source: CyBerCorp, Inc.

1. Stock box with Level II data for the stock we are looking at
2. One-minute candlestick chart for S&P Futures
3. One-minute candlestick chart for Nasdaq 100 futures
4. 300-Day daily candlestick chart linked to the stock box
5. Five-minute intraday candlestick chart linked to the stock box.

As soon as we enter a stock in the stock box, we immediately have access to the five-minute candlestick data as well as its daily chart. A picture of our computer screen is shown in Figure 5.15.

How Many Shares Should You Buy?
The wonderful thing about playing a consolidation-breakout strategy is that stocks that break out tend to have significant price moves after long consolidations. You can estimate its potential for further movement by observing how far the stock has moved in its initial run.

If we see a stock that tends to increase about five points after consolidations, we may only buy 200 shares. We prefer to buy 200 shares and then sell 100 after the stock has gained 1–2 points. Because we have now booked some profit, we can be more patient with the remaining 100 shares. We will let that 100 shares ride as long as we feel that the stock still has upward momentum and ride out a few wiggles. We will initially keep the original stop on the remaining 100 shares, which was set at a price immediately below the low of the consolidation range. Psychologically, it helps us to know that we are profitable. Then when the stock moves up but hits resistance and goes through a minor retracement, we are psychologically able to stay in the trade and give it a chance to resume its upward movement.

If the stock is strong and continues moving up until it starts a new consolidation at a higher level than the first consolidation, we change our stop to a price immediately below the bottom of the second consolidation. In Figure 5.11, we bought 200 shares of HLTH when the stock broke above the first consolidation and traded at $47^5/_8$. When the stock traded at $48^5/_8$, we sold 100 shares but kept our original stop that was set at $47^3/_{16}$ (one-eighth below the low of the first consolida-

figure 5.15   display of trading computer screen used for consolidation breakouts

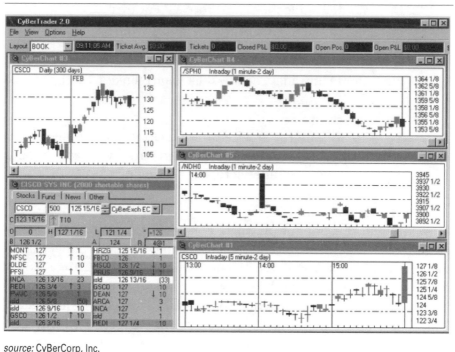

source: CyBerCorp, Inc.

tion). When the stock consolidated again with a new consolidation range of 48³/₄ to 49¹/₈, we changed the stop of our remaining 100 shares to 48⁵/₈, one-eighth below the low of the new consolidation range. We have now booked profits on the first 100 shares and insured a profit of at least one point on the remaining 100 shares because we will make no less than one point on the remaining 100 shares (stop of 48⁵/₈ minus entry of 47⁵/₈). We are now profitable and can stay long in the stock until we see signs that the stock has started to reverse direction.

where to find stocks for consolidation breakouts
Over time, you will find your favorite approaches to finding stocks that are in consolidations and potentially ready to break out. We will share with you a few that we use to help you get started.

Briefing.com is an excellent resource. If accessed directly at www.briefing.com, there is a small monthly fee charged for the service. Many on-line brokers will give you access to briefing.com through their Web sites free of charge if you are a customer of that brokerage, so we suggest you check with any on-line brokers that you may use for your investment accounts. The "In Play" section will give you key stocks in the news and stocks that are showing significant gains or losses for the day.

Day-trading software typically gives you access to a list of NYSE and Nasdaq top gainers and losers. This is a great starting point to find stocks that are moving up or down during the day. Remember, stocks that have had strong movement during the day will usually go through consolidations before they resume their movement later in the day.

The Informational Web sites listed in Chapter 7 are a great resource for finding stocks that are on the move. We have included numerous sites that have summaries of stocks that are gaining or losing ground for the day. Find the stocks that have had movement and keep watching them until you see consolidations. Scan, Scan, Scan.

Find sectors that are strong and look for stocks within those sectors. If one stock in a sector is moving up strongly, another stock in that sector may be consolidating and getting ready for its upward movement. Understand which stocks are in the same sector because they will often move up or down in tandem, but with some time lag so that the behavior of one can help predict the upcoming behavior of another.

a warning on shorting consolidations

When a stock has been moving upward and then consolidates, you would be looking for a break to occur in the direction of the original trend, so you would be looking for a breakout in order to go long. Similarly, when a stock has been moving downward, you would be looking for a breakout to occur in order to go short. Although this is theoretically what occurs, we want to caution all new part-time traders against going short until you have substantial experience trading. Shorting consolidations that appear to be breaking downward can be very dangerous.

When a stock has good news, it will often go up all day long. It may gap up, then move up from the open, consolidate, and continue to move up all day. But when a stock has bad news, the pattern can be different. If the news is really bad, it can fall drastically immediately until it finds some level of support and then gradually recovers some of its loss during the day.

In addition, even if a stock looks like it is drifting down, it may have significant levels of support all along the way. So the drops may not be as substantial as you would need in order to have a profitable trade. When going long on a strong stock, particularly one that has broken to all-time new highs, there is no upward price resistance, but when going short, the stock has previously been at those lower prices and has established multiple price supports along the way.

This is not to say that it is impossible to short down-trending stocks that are currently in consolidations. However, we warn you that the procedure is more dangerous than going long in upward trends. It is also difficult to execute a short after the break has occurred because you can't short a stock without an increase in the bid, or an uptick. This doesn't always happen in a rapidly falling stock. When it does occur, then you are in a dilemma about whether the stock has already fallen too much to be worth entering the trade. When you are new to trading, practice going long before you attempt shorting, and when you do decide to short, learn by only going short on consolidation breakouts that have been called by a reputable trading room like Swingtrader.net.

SureStart ⟩ Swingtrader trading room for consolidation-breakout strategy

One of the best places to find great calls on intraday consolidations is in the Swingtrader trading room, accessed through www.swingtrader.net. One of the room leaders specializes in finding and calling entries on consolidations. This leader is particularly thorough at researching the behavior of each stock on a daily basis, of analyzing its daily and intraday support and resistance, and at giving clear, concise entry and exit points for each trade, and this leader always gives the recommended stop for each trade. This is a great place to learn and a great place to supplement your own hunt for stocks that are consolidating!

some final words to ensure your success with our trading strategies

Practice, practice, and practice in simulation trading!

Do not be greedy; take your profits!

Exit a trade when you can, not when you have to!

Take your preset stop loss without hesitation!

Do not stray too far from the root of your successful trading strategy!

We wish all part-time trading associates success.

The following section provides books and Web sites that can provide information about consolidation-breakout strategies and the special areas they cover best. Additional information on the books is in the bibliography.

Resources for Short-Term Momentum and Consolidation-Breakout Trading Strategies

Japanese Candlestick Charting Techniques, Steve Nison
This book covers candlesticks, higher lows, and lower highs.

Introduction to Technical Analysis, Martin Pring
This book covers a wide range of material, including Bollinger bands, candlesticks, higher lows (in "Peak and Trough Analysis"), lower highs (In "Peak and Trough Analysis"), moving averages, price support and resistance, oscillators (in "Principles of Momentum"), stochastics, and volume.

The Electronic Day Trader, Marc Friedfertig and George West
Look here for information on money management, Nasdaq 100 futures, and S&P futures.

Stock Patterns for Day Trading, Barry Rudd
Consolidation breakouts and price support and resistance are two areas covered particularly well in this book.

Trading for a Living, Dr. Alexander Elder
This is a worthwhile title to look through for a better grasp of Bollinger bands, money management, moving averages, oscillators (in "Momentum"), volume, and price support and resistance.

www.clearstation.com/education
Try this Web site for information about moving averages, oscillators, price support and resistance, shorting or selling short, stochastics, and volume.

www.undergroundtrader.com
We think this Web site is a worthwhile source if you want to increase your understanding about moving averages, Nasdaq futures, shorting or selling short, S&P futures, and stochastics.

www.swingtrader.net
We've mentioned this Web site earlier in this book. It is a good place to go to find out more about consolidation breakouts.

www.tradingmarkets.com
This Web site specializes in consolidations, moving averages, price support and resistance, short selling, and volume.

chapter 6

money management

protecting your capital

We can't state this often enough: The object of day trading is to turn a profit on your investment. In order to do that you must protect the capital with which you are working.

margin accounts

New part-time traders must be cautious of some not-so-apparent risks associated with trading. Most traders will be opening an account that is called a margin account on a two-for-one basis. This means that when you open your account, with $10,000, for an example, you have the buying power of $20,000. This sounds good and, yes it is good. However if it is not properly respected, one could get in trouble.

Day-trading margin accounts are usually fully usable during the day, even with buying and selling the same stock over and over again. However, when it comes to holding a stock overnight, one should diligently read the overnight margin requirements. Do this before you start trading. Many if not most brokerage companies allow less margin on holding stocks overnight on some of the more volatile stocks, such as Internet companies, because anything can happen and does happen overnight. A stock could plunge 10, 20, 30 points and more.

Let's look at what might happen to you and the brokerage company if there were a sudden drop in a stock's price overnight and your account were fully margined out. Say you bought XYZ stock for $20 a share. You bought the full amount of shares that you could with your $10,000 account margined at two to one. This would be 1,000 shares for a total cost of $20,000. Overnight the stock has bad news, which could be a report of bad earnings, a discovery of unacceptable business practices, the CEO resigns, and so on. Anyway, the stock drops to $5.00 a share. Guess what? You now owe your broker $5,000 within three days! You will receive a formal notice known as a margin call, so get that $5,000 to send in to your broker and pray that the stock goes no lower.

Now, this can also happen during trading hours. Very bad news on the stock that you own comes out and you are fully margined as in the foregoing example. You went out for lunch or you went back to work with the intention of checking on your stock later. You come back and find yourself out $5,000 just like the overnight guy. We bring this up to show you some worst-case scenarios. As a part-time trader we would not expect you to be leaving your chair when you have an open position in a trade. Also this shows that you must use exceptional caution whenever you use your margin. Let this serve as another reminder to keep your stop losses.

So now let's go back to why you must read your broker's overnight margin requirements. You are fully margined on buying the 1,000 shares of XZY stock as in the aforementioned example. You have used up your $10,000 and the broker's $10,000. You have not read the overnight margin rules. You wake up the next morning and your stock is still at the same price, but you get a notice from your broker telling you that you have a margin call; you will have to get the money to them in three days or sell the stock because you are under a margin call. You have a margin call in this example because you did not read that the overnight margin allowed on Internet stocks is only 50 percent of your cash account or, in this case, you could only use $5,000 of your broker's funds holding an Internet stock overnight.

This all could get worse if the stock starts dropping and your margin call increases. So please, before you start trading know what the overnight margin requirements are and do not go into an overnight hold beyond what your overnight margin allows. To protect themselves as well as protecting you, brokerage margin may be reduced by 50 percent or more for overnight holds on some stocks.

shorting or short selling

Not all traders feel comfortable shorting or selling borrowed stock. There is a good reason for caution by part-time traders. Shorting a stock or a short sale is selling a stock not owned by the trader. This occurs by borrowing the stock from the broker with the intent of replacing the stock at a lower price than it was borrowed. The profit to the trader is the difference in the shorting price and the price to which stock falls and the trader repurchases the stock. When the stock is repurchased, it is called covering the short. Should the stock rise in price after shorting it, the trader will have a loss should he buy it back at a price higher than the shorting price.

Shorting a stock is only possible on an uptick, an increase of the bid from the previous inside bid. This doesn't always happen when a stock is falling rapidly. When it does occur, you are in a dilemma about whether the stock has already fallen too much to be worth entering the trade.

Shorting a stock is going against the emotional exuberance most traders have for trading, namely watching a stock rise, not fall. We highly suggest that part-time traders thoroughly learn and profit from going long before learning the techniques of shorting. We have listed resources that discuss shorting in detail at the end of "Short-Term Momentum Trading Strategies" in Chapter 5.

You should also be aware that shorting losses potentially have no limit. When going long or buying a stock, the most you can lose is the value of the stock. So if you bought a 1,000 shares of a $20 stock, the most you could lose would be $20,000. However, if you short 1,000 shares of a $20 stock and, after all the markets are closed, super good news comes, you may find your stock up 40 points! You could conceivably have a $40,000 loss on your hands. In addition to this, you might even consider holding the stock a little longer hoping that it will come back down. Guess what. Other short holders of this stock are waking up and saying, "Wow, I better buy now before it goes higher and I have a greater loss." This is when things get worse for you. It is called the short squeeze.

A short squeeze occurs when the holders of a short sale are faced with their stock's rapid rise, causing many of these short holders to cover their losses and forcing the price of the stock to go even higher. The remaining short holders are squeezed by having their losses increase until they, too, cover their short position by buying the stock back. This increase in buying by shorters adds to the price increase in the stock.

We hope this information will be well heeded. Be cautious with your margin account and shorting.

reducing your risks

We strongly encourage you to plan a trading budget once you are in the later stage of your simulation trading. If you start at this point, you will carry it forward into your live trading. Keep your budget simple.

First, establish an overall maximum allowance for losses that will tell you it's time to think of some alternative part-time business. Stick with whatever amount you have chosen. To alter this amount of acceptable loss further once you have reached your limit would only compound a bad situation.

Second, set a figure for a one-day loss. When you reach this figure, stop trading for the day! Take a break and review your mistakes. If you have several down days in a row, you may wish to take a few days off to focus on your overall trading strategy to see what went wrong and what you can do to improve your strategy.

Third, know what your stop loss will be on every trade before you enter! A good method for doing this would be to preset your stop loss, for example at one-quarter point for each short-term momentum trade. In addition to this, establish a dollar stop loss amount per trade. Determine how many shares you can purchase so that you can hold your stop loss and not exceed your total dollar value stop loss.

Let's use an example. In this case you have a trade stop loss of one-quarter point per share and a total stop loss of $200 per trade. Before you enter the trade you calculate that you can hold 800 shares through a one-quarter point loss and not exceed your per-trade dollar stop loss of $200. ($200 / $.25 = 800 shares, i.e., divide your per-trade stop loss by your per-share stop loss). Remember, there will be times when you will see your trade not going your way before you have reached your stop loss. No use hoping for a change, just get out and be ready for the next trade.

By keeping stop losses for each trade and a daily stop loss basis, you reduce your risk of losing control of your emotions along with your trading skills. Respect your trading budget and it will help you become a better trader.

stop loss—the key to preserving your capital

A *stop loss* is the maximum loss you will allow. By contrast a *stop* is the price where you will exit a trade if the trade goes against you.

If you set a *stop loss* at one-quarter point, your *stop* will be set at a price one-quarter point below your entry price if going long. The reverse is true for shorting a stock.

You must always know your *stop loss* before you enter any trade. We have italicized the words *stop loss* and *stop* because of the importance of this action to a trader.

If success in the trading of short-term momentum stocks hinges on any one discipline, it is your ability to take stops. The consistency with which you take stops is the best indicator of your discipline. If this indicator is warning you about your discipline, it may be time to reconsider trading as a viable business for you. Every trader, whether experienced or a novice, will have losses. Profitability comes to those of you who cut your losses short. When you do so, you preserve your working capital. The failure to take predetermined stop losses results in the failure of most traders.

Stops and Stop Losses for Short-Term Momentum Trading
In a conservative stock such as CSCO you may wish to hold a very tight stop loss, say one-eighth below your entry level. In a conservative mode of trading off the one-minute stochastic bounce we would suggest

an attempt at buying at the bid price. If you get in on the inside bid price, you are not already "down" one price level from the inside ask price and you are not paying the "spread," the difference between the bid and the ask price. With a stock such as CSCO, you will usually see many market makers and ECNs on any given price level on the bid and ask. This affords you liquidity to exit a trade should you see a reversal in price starting.

Example of implementing a stop loss:

You buy CSCO with a one-eighth-point stop loss, meaning that if the price of CSCO drops one-eighth point below your purchase price, you sell. A one-eighth-point loss is the largest loss you will take. The inside bid and ask are:

CSCO bid $59^{15}/_{16}$ CSCO ask 60

You bid $59^{15}/_{16}$ for CSCO and you are filled. You now own CSCO at $59^{15}/_{16}$. You know that your stop price is $59^{13}/_{16}$. That is the price at which you will sell, which is one-eighth point below your purchase price. Unfortunately, soon after you bought CSCO, the prices change:

CSCO bid $59^{7}/_{8}$ CSCO ask $59^{15}/_{16}$

You are now watching the bid and ask closely. A few minutes later the prices change again:

CSCO bid $59^{13}/_{16}$ CSCO ask $59^{7}/_{8}$

You are now down on the bid, one-eighth point below your purchase price and at your predetermined stop of $59^{13}/_{16}$. Without hesitation, you sell CSCO to the bidder at $59^{13}/_{16}$. You are out with a one-eighth-point loss. With 1,000 shares, this is a loss of $125 plus commissions for a total loss of approximately $165. CSCO continues down. You smile. You have just done what is so difficult for many traders to do: You took your predetermined stop loss.

This is a simple example of taking a stop loss. Some of you may be asking: why didn't you sell at the ask and only lose a one-sixteenth point? Why not wait until your stop loss price was at the ask, so if the price came back up, you would still be in the trade? Yes, you could have done either before you took your stop loss, depending on how many buyers and sellers were there and depending on other market indicators. With experience you will know what your chances are for getting out on the ask with your stop loss. You will know how to hold onto your shares until the last second to get out, so if CSCO decides to move up from a low bid of $59^{13}/_{16}$ you will still be in the trade. However, right now as a new part-time trader, you are in the learning phase, and you want to keep your losses to a minimum. When a stock turns against you and your stop loss is reached, you want to make sure you get out. In this case the surest way out is to take the bid price at your predetermined stop loss.

A Real-Life Incident
We had just started trading CSCO. On the day prior to trading, we knew that CSCO was a slow mover, and didn't think CSCO really moved up or down that much on any given day. We went into CSCO long with some vague thoughts about taking a one-quarter-point stop loss on this trade if necessary. CSCO started dropping and reached the stop loss point we had set. We thought, "Well, we'll hold a little longer. It's going to come back up." Next thing we knew, CSCO is down one-half. The loss is now $500. Too much. We decided to hold. We went through a painful afternoon hoping the stock would come back and watched as it dropped $2^{1}/_{2}$ points. Near the close of the market, we had to make a decision about whether to hold overnight. We considered breaking a cardinal rule of day traders: do not take home losing positions. We decided we couldn't sell because we had taken too much of a loss. We held the stock overnight.

The next morning CSCO and tech stocks in general were gapping down from their close, and the S&P futures were down big. Because we had the majority of our working capital in this trade, we needed the capital back to trade. With both factors under consideration, CSCO was sold for an approximate three-point loss or $3,000. Why? Because we did not take a one-quarter point or $250 stop loss. CSCO, by the way, continued down for over two weeks in a market sell off, so you just never know. We sincerely hope that you can appreciate the need to take predetermined stop losses to preserve your capital. If you can't do it, stop trading.

Once you start your educational process, you will learn that not all *stops* are the same. Different stocks, trading strategies, and market conditions warrant different size stop losses.

the role of your trading diary

Your trade journal, trade diary, or log are all the same and a very important educational tool in your journey to becoming a successful part-time trader. Let your diary speak to you, let it show you your weaknesses and your strength as a trader. Then use what it says to improve your success!

Your diary for each trade can be very simple. In fact, we suggest you keep it simple so that you will not be discouraged from keeping it. If you try to keep too much data, you will falter in diligently keeping your diary, and it will become a worthless tool. We believe it best that you record your notes concerning your trade immediately after the trade has been closed, while all the data concerning the trade is in front of you, such as charts and Time of Sales (TOS).

As we discussed in "Simulation Trading," in Chapter 4, you need to have rules and a trading plan established to give you guidance during your learning curve. Once you have the rules and trading plan in place, you should note in your journal where you deviated from either or both of these and the results. Likewise, you will record what occurs when you followed both.

There will be times that you will follow both your trading plan and all your rules, yet you still have a losing trade. Look to see why it was not a winning trade. Compare your trade with previous entries for similar losses. Your diary may be able to alert you to changes that are needed in your trading plan and/or rules. If everything checks out, continue with your present trading strategy; losses will occur even when you do everything right.

For winning trades, your diary will tell you what you are doing right. Perhaps you think you can do better if you change your rules a little. Your diary will tell you how the changes have affected your overall results.

What to Watch For

In the general comments of your diary, we suggest you pay particular attention to your pre-set stop losses or trailing stop losses. Are you holding them? Check each trade to see whether you are doing so. Are you taking profits where you said you would? Were you totally focused on your trading? Were you entering the trade on your own analysis or based on someone else's call? Was it a keyboard error? Are you going against the general market trend? Were you chasing a stock?

Your trading journal will help you improve your trading strategies and help you implement tighter discipline in following those rules you are breaking repetitively. At the end of the day, week, and month, compare successes or failures on each trade to your written trading plan and rules. How do they match up? Where do you need to make adjustments? What mistakes are repetitive? What time of day are you making the most successful trades? What stocks are you most successful with? What share size are you best at handling emotionally?

If your diary shows that you are less successful with large share lots, you need to understand the reasons behind this. You may feel more stress in handling these trades and/or you may be having difficulty in routing and executing large share lots.

Following is a list of those items you need to track when keeping a diary:

Date

Day

Stock

Long or short

Time of entry

Time of exit

Share lot attempted

Lot fill

Gain or loss points

Gain or loss $

Notes

Day P&L

Everyone's diary will be a little different. When we are short-term momentum trading, we like to look at the gains in terms of points. This is more meaningful to us, but for our emotional gratification we like to look at the dollar amount. If you are holding a stock overnight, you might add a category indicating how much the stock was up in the last half hour of trading. You might also want a category listing the price premarket at 8:00 A.M. EST the following morning.

Sample Trade Journal on a Not-So-Good Day
This sample from our journal was taken during the beginning of our learning curve.

Date Day	Stock L or S	Shares Filled	Entry Exit	Time	P&L pts.	Notes
2-5 Fri	CIEN L	200 (100)	$26^1/_8$ $25^7/_8$	9:38 9:45	$<^3/_8>$ <$91.58>	Breakout. Play called by another person in trading room. **Trade on what you know not off of others.**
2-5 Fri	LCOS L	200 (200)	$137^3/_8$ 137	10:01 10:02	$<^3/_8>$ <$121.32>	News. Stock already up big off stochs. **Evaluate news,** This was news in premarket. **Do not buy high up on stochs!**
2-5 Fri	NAVR L	1000 1000	$20^1/_8$ $20^3/_{16}$	10:17 10:19	$^1/_8$ $50.20	Reversal of stochs off bottom. Just in and out. Good.
2-5 Fri	CIEN L	1000 1000	$24^{15}/_{16}$ $24^{13}/_{16}$	14:47 14:51	$<^1/_8>$ <$172.24>	Reversal. Stochs already up to 20 from

Date Day	Stock L or S	Shares Filled	Entry Exit	Time	P&L pts.	Notes
						0, 3 minute MA in down trend. Going against trend, very bad. **Do not go against trend!**
2-5	CIEN	1000	24³/₄	14:55	<¹/₈>	
Fri	L	1000	24⁵/₈	15:06	<$171.48>	Reversal. Once again trying to catch a falling knife. **Stochs had not bounced. Do not go against the trend. Learn or quit!**
Daily P&L					<$506.42>	

Key: Profit and Loss (P&L) is after commission expense. Stochastics = stochs; Moving averages = MA; Bollinger bands = BB; Reversal = stocks going from down to up or going from up to down.

Sample Trade Journal on a Good Day
This sample entry comes after many more months of learning and trading.

Date Day	Stock L or S	Shares Filled	Entry Exit	Time	P&L pts.	Notes
10-5	CSCO	500	71³/₈	9:55	³/₈	
Tue	L	(500)	71³/₄	10:00	$147.60	Breakout, not my usual play, gapped open then flat. Fed day.
10-5	CSCO	500	72⁹/₁₆	11:33	³/₈	
Tue	S	(500)	72³/₁₆	11:38	$147.60	Reversal, stochs coming down S&P big time off 100 Stochs Continued sell off to 71⁷/₈.
10-5	CSCO	500	72⁹/₁₆	13:36	<³/₁₆>	

Date Day	Stock L or S	Shares Filled	Entry Exit	Time	P&L pts.	Notes
Tues	S	(500)	72³/₄	13:38	<$133.65>	Reversal off S&P and CSCO100 stochs. Not sustained, ok followed rules, took stop loss.
10-5 Tue	CSCO S	1000 (-0-)				No fill on Fed announcement even though set for ISLD hit.
10-5	CSCO	1000	71³/₄	14:24	³/₈	Sell off. Not greedy, dangerous turf, in & out.
10-5 Tue	CSCO S	1000 (1000)	71³/₄ 71¹/₄	14:34 14:38	¹/₂ $460.10	Mid range stochs but trend in BB and MA all down on charts, Mkt. Down. Continued on down. Not greedy!
10-5 Tues	CSCO L	500 (500)	70¹/₂ 71¹/₈	15:14 15:29	⁵/₈ $272.60	Reversal off stochs for S&Ps & CSCO. Continued up for day.
Daily P&L					$1,229.35	

Note: This was a good day to be a day trader. Very distinct chart patterns off reversals. The Fed news on interest rates made for volatile stock movements and high volume. This is all good for the trader.

Changes Resulting from Keeping a Diary
You will note that the first journal shown is quite different from the last. Based on the journal analysis, we made changes in our trading that made us more successful. Those include the following:

Trade the same stock over and over and become familiar with its rhythm, market makers, resistance and support levels on a daily,

weekly, and longer term. Noticed that on February 5, three different stocks were traded. None of these stocks were traded in the
days prior to February 5 nor after that date. On the other hand,
we traded CSCO consistently day after day in October.

In February, trades were being made off the news. If you are not
sure if the news is *new* news, don't trade on it. To solve mistakes
on news plays, news plays for a quick scalp were eliminated. We
now use the news to confirm trends developing on the charts.

One of the biggest changes made was narrowing our strategy to
buying stocks on the one-minute stochastic bounce from the
zero band, and shorting stocks on the one-minute stochastic
bounce from the 100 band. This is used in conjunction with similar stochastic bounces occurring in the S&P and Nasdaq futures,
as well as some additional indicators. In February, reversals were
more of a gut feeling. We were not being disciplined and waiting
for the zero or 100-band stochastic bounce. The journal clearly
shows which is the successful strategy.

Going against the trend. What can we say, but don't do it. After
seeing the words **Do not go against the trend** in the journal
enough times, it stuck!

Trading based exclusively on other people's calls is a bad habit.
You will not learn how to trade, and you will not progress on your
own if your strategy is following someone else's call. This is not a
sound strategy. If someone alerts you to a stock, look at it and do
your own analysis. It is good to know what stocks and sectors are
moving. If the call fits into your trading parameters and rules, go
ahead and consider it. If it is a momentum stock with action, you
may wait for it to fit your type of trading strategy.

Since those days in February, we have not played other's calls
without thought. The journal showed repeatedly that these
were losing trades. There were many reasons and factors behind this, but the primary problem was that they were fast-
moving stocks on breakout plays. Breakout plays are not suited
for everyone, particularly on fast-moving stocks. (Consolidation-

breakout plays are entirely different and much safer than these plays.)

What is missing in the February journal were the words, "Take your stop loss!" At that time, the discipline to take stop losses was weak. After repeatedly making the same mistake of not keeping a tight *stop loss* and suffering the consequential losses, it finally "sunk in" and became part of my discipline.

Keep your journal even when you are winning consistently. It keeps you alert to your successful trading strategies and rules.

the psychology of trading or, why am I doing these stupid things?

We cannot overemphasize the importance of understanding your conscious and subconscious motivations that influence your trading.

who is running your ship?

"How could I have done that?" Sooner or later you will hear yourself saying this. Puzzlement at your own actions! Confusion! Trading will either teach you more things about the workings of your inner mind or you will quit trading, wondering what ever made you do the things you do.

We are not psychologists, so we can't profess to give you the underlying psychology of what occurs. All we can do is share our experience and hope that you can learn something from what you read. We have both been involved in a number of different careers—marketing consulting, real estate, engineering, research and development, quality management—a broad gamut of fields where we have worked and been successful. We know how to set goals, create strategies, develop plans, and successfully implement those plans. We know how to be successful. But nothing prepared us for the experience of trading and the experience of failure.

If there is one thing that differentiates trading from most professions, it is that trading is primarily controlled by your subconscious mind, not your conscious mind. To trade successfully, you must discover the role your subconscious mind is playing in your behavior. You must understand its motivations and bring those motivations forward into your conscious mind where they can be dealt with and where they no longer have the ability to sabotage your behavior.

This probably makes no sense to you; so let me explain the experience one of us went through as we began day trading.

A Story from Jeanette

After several months of studying, trading, gaining skills, and making significant strides in my progress, my trading suddenly took a turn for the worse. My behavior started to diverge from my rules, and my rules seemed to get lost each morning in the passion of trading. The best analogy I can give is one of dieting—starting out the day saying, "This is the day I begin the wonderful, healthy diet with the complete exercise program," then somewhere around noon scooping out some ice cream or deciding to nap instead of going to the gym. When you do not follow through with your planned diet or exercise program, it is disheartening, confusing. You don't understand how you could feel so totally committed the night before, yet give up all the best plans the very next day. Upsetting, yes, but nowhere near as destructive as a day of trading when you have thrown all your rules out the window.

So you carefully draft a long list of trading rules—rules you are committed to live with, that you believe in, that came from your own mind, based on your study and your research. One may be your commitment to keeping a tight stop loss, maybe one-quarter point maximum on 500 shares, so you enter the trade long when you believe positive momentum has hit the stock. Perhaps you see a breakout play. But things change, you are now wrong and there are signs that the stock is either not moving up or, worse yet, starting to move down. It drops one-eighth point and your mind says maybe this is a wiggle. It drops one-quarter point and your mind says, "probably a wiggle, I don't want to sell now—

look at the commission I am wasting if it is just a wiggle." It is now down three-eighths of a point; you have passed your stop loss and you are on the losing side of a trade. You put in a sell order, but the order isn't filled at the limit of the current bid because the stock is now dropping like a falling knife, and everyone is trying to get out at the same time. I watch it drop. Down, down, down—oh, my! it is now down three-quarters of a point—way, way past my stop loss. Now I am married to the stock. I can't bear three-quarters of a point on 500 shares. My mind starts reviewing the stock's history; surely it will have a retracement from any sharp decline—if not today, surely tomorrow. It is now down one point. I am sick and I am scared—maybe it won't retrace. Maybe it will fall further today. The pain is severe. I want to cry or scream. I no longer have faith in retracement or belief in tomorrow. I need to stop the pain, so I put in a market order to sell. I am out—down $1\frac{1}{8}$ on 500 shares. And then I watch the stock start to reverse. It is going up, but I am not in it anymore. I have taken a loss, a big loss. I am feeling sick. I don't trust this stock anymore, so I don't capitalize on its retracement. I hate this stock. I hate myself. I hate trading. I am looking at my rules about taking an automatic one-quarter point stop loss and wondering, why, Oh, why, didn't I follow that rule? How did this happen to me? Worse yet, how did it happen again, because this is becoming a pattern. I am doing the same stupid thing over and over. I stop trading, sit in a comfortable chair, and decide to analyze my behavior. I will learn from this mistake. I will understand why it happened and then I will never do it again. After all, I am an intelligent woman, a success in many fields, so how did I turn into such a turkey, such a dope? Why am I making this mistake over and over and not learning from my experiences? I continue to beat myself up, but I get nowhere.

This is where I found myself, and this is where many, if not most traders, find themselves somewhere fairly early in their trading careers. We know what to do, we write tight rules of what we must do, we know we are intelligent because we have been highly successful in other careers, yet we find ourselves completely at the mercy of some inner demon that makes us do stupid things in our trading. And we have no clue of how to change this, because it is not at all understandable.

It was during this time that I decided I needed help from outside of myself; I needed more understanding of this inner process that was having such a big affect on my trading. I remembered that people had recommended the book, *The Disciplined Trader*. I had even purchased the book months before and read one chapter, but this time I opened the book and committed to not only reading it but also to doing all the exercises recommended by the author. It took a lot of time and a lot of effort. It was difficult, but it taught me things about myself that I wasn't aware of. It brought to the surface my subconscious thoughts and desires, which had been sabotaging my conscious efforts at trading.

One of the things I learned was that I was conflicted about whether trading met my personal needs. In my other careers, I had always been involved with people, and I had always assumed the role of teacher and mentor to people in my work environment. This was extremely important to me, and it was a big part of how I saw myself as a person. I hadn't found any way to do that in my trading career. In fact, trading was rather isolating—me, myself, and I were my work environment. My subconscious mind was telling me it wasn't too happy about it. Now, you will find that your subconscious mind is always out for what is best for you, its only purpose is to make you happy. In my case, it thought I would be happier being back around people, mentoring, doing my old thing. It wanted to make me happy quickly, and my subconscious thought that the way to get me back with people, back to mentoring was to make me stop trading. What better way to do that than to have me fail at trading? It tricked me into ignoring stop-loss rules, knowing that the end result would be devastating failure, therefore, a return to a career around people. My subconscious decided that it would make me fail at trading so I could succeed at being with people and mentoring. It wanted to make me happy.

I can imagine that many of you are rolling your eyes right now, thinking that I am perhaps a little loco. Trust me here. If you have ever gone off a diet, not exercised when you promised yourself you would, not done any disciplined thing that you promised yourself you would do, then you, too, have experienced your subconscious taking control at the expense of your conscious mind. And that is what happens in trading, but it happens with such severe financial impact that you cannot afford to ignore it. You must understand what is going on. You must bring the issues to the surface and show your subconscious that you know what you want and need, and show it that you will be responsible for getting what you need. It doesn't have to take over.

In my situation, by going through the exercises in the book, I uncovered this issue, became aware of how important it was to me, and decided to take conscious control. I determined a path of interacting with more people while trading by increasing my participation after hours in a trading room, and I even began mentoring people after hours in the trading room. I needed to mentor; it was part of my self-image. When I returned to this increased people interaction, began a new program for mentoring, my trading got back on track. I was able to consciously control my trading. My subconscious didn't have to take control.

As you read about traders, you will notice an amazing amount of introspection among successful traders. Successful traders must know themselves and their motivations. They must understand why they are trading and what they want out of trading. The more they understand themselves, the more they explore their own truth, the less likely their subconscious minds will take over and the less likely hidden fears or desires will sabotage them.

So, how do you know when you have an issue with your subconscious? A big clue is that you are suddenly making frequent, stupid decisions. I am not talking bad decisions made from lack of training. I am talking about decisions that go against your best judgment. You have decided to hold to a one-quarter point stop loss and you just sold with a loss of three-quarters of a point. You have a strategy of sticking to slow-moving stocks, like Dell or CSCO, and you just jumped into opening day of an Internet IPO (even if you made money, this is a problem if it goes against your strategy). Basically, any time you are not doing what you have written down in your strategy or your rules, you are not trading fully consciously. Your subconscious is in control. That means trouble.

what are you focusing on?

Intense self-analysis is vital and will help you determine your deeper motivations and let you take control of your trading with your conscious mind—the only part of your mind that has any business trading. But some of your trading problems will be focused much more short term than that. It is not all about your long-term dreams and fears; often something happening in the moment will be enough to wreck your trading.

Anything that distracts you from trading is dangerous. One of us had major home renovations that had to be done over a period of several months. On any particular day, repairmen would show up and start hammering. If you really believe you can trade sensibly when people are hammering on your house, we beg to differ! Focusing on trading means 100 percent focus, thinking exclusively about timing for entering a trade and exiting a trade. If part of your mind is involved in wondering whether someone is showing up to finish some work or in answering periodic questions from repairmen, then the total mind is not involved in trading, and the results will reflect that.

Our best advice is to know yourself. If you can concentrate fully regardless of who is around you, then you are a fortunate person indeed. But if you get distracted, look up, lose your train of thought, then you must always be careful. Analyze your surroundings. Are they quiet enough? Will you be interrupted when you are in a trade? Will the kids be walking in the door after school asking a million questions? Will the phone be ringing and will you feel obliged to answer it? Be truthful with yourself about how much distraction you can personally deal with. Your trading will reveal the truth. And if you are distracted, your trading will suffer. So, if the room is too noisy, if you are expecting commotion from any source, do yourself a favor and take the day off from trading. If you feel guilty taking the day off from trading, spend the day studying. But never, ever trade if you can't focus 100 percent on the trading.

your self-confidence is more fragile than you think

It is so easy to lose focus for a few seconds and end up losing money. The real danger of repeating this too often is not the lost money. It is the lost confidence. A little lost money we can explain away—the cost of doing business, the learning curve. However, if it happens repeatedly, you will no longer believe in yourself, and lost confidence will lead to hesitation. You will lose the edge that is so very important in day trading—the ability to think quickly and act quickly.

The only real cure for lost self-confidence is reestablishing a belief in yourself by establishing a series of mini-successes—successful trades and successful and consistent implementation of your own rules. Go back again to simulation trading or paper trading with your rules and your personal strategy clearly in mind. Your diary will tell you that you are following your own rules and that you can be successful. Then return to real trading with very small shares—you do not need to make money here, you need to make good decisions and acknowledge those decisions. Again, your diary will help tell you that you are doing well and that you are consistent. Then you can believe in yourself once again.

is it possible that I am greedy?

I never thought of myself as a greedy person. Money has never been all that important to me. I always preferred the concept of having a simple life. My primary goal for day trading was to have the luxury of giving away money once my basic needs were met, so you can imagine my surprise when I found that greed was a controlling force in my behavior when trading. Each of you needs to understand this and to look for signs that it might be influencing your behavior. It will make you do bad things that will hurt your profitability. Until you see that you are capable of greed, you will not take steps to protect yourself from it.

beware of cyber locker rooms

Scenario: I am trading while participating in a chat room. Next to my keyboard is my personal list of rules and strategies that I am committed to follow when trading. On this particular day, I have been following my rules, trading conservatively, and have made a nice, comfortable profit for the day. My own personal rule says that I will *never* enter a breakout at the high of the day's prices unless that breakout occurs after the stock has been consolidating within a tight range for a significant period of time. But the trading-room leader really loves breakout plays and has personal success with them. (Remember, always, that trading is very personal and you must find out what *you* are good at.)

Now, I have been making one-quarter to one-half point gains on each of my trades, and they are very respectable profits. Even with 500 shares, it doesn't take too many trades like that to support a very comfortable lifestyle. But, while doing my own thing quietly, I have also been watching the action in the room. A hot Initial Public Offering (IPO) has opened and tons of people have played it one or more times. Wow, the last time the play was called in the room, some people were hooting and howling because they made seven points. I say to myself, "Jeanette, you know you don't do IPOs." Then a breakout play is called. Again, I see people cheering because they made one to two points. So much cyber slapping on the back is going on that I feel like I am in a cyber locker room. I am trying to ignore it, trying to stay focused on my own personal strategies, but frankly, I am getting annoyed. I am angry at the frenzy—or that's what I attribute my displeasure to. Why can't everyone just keep quiet so I can pay attention to what the moderator is saying? I think I am having trouble concentrating, but the next time a breakout play is called—oh, my goodness—I am in it! And it falls. I lose money. I can't keep my stop because I am so confused about why I am in this play at all—this is the play where I *always* lose money. Why did I enter?

greed!

Greed catalyzed by frenzy. Group mentality. For the same reason that when I go to a football game, even though I don't follow football, if the entire stadium is screaming "Touchdown," I am up screaming as well. No matter how independent we are, we are still human and subject to human frailties, and there is some psychological quirk that makes us behave as part of a group when the emotions of the group become highly charged. We become part of a herd. If that herd is heading somewhere we hadn't planned on going, we are very likely to go there anyway.

How did this group get so highly charged emotionally? What is this emotion that is ripping through the group? And how in the world can you get so emotionally charged up from reading the lines in a chat room? This doesn't sound possible, but it is very possible and very likely.

Let me discuss first how the emotions can be so contagious when you are only reading a dialogue from a chat room. Trading is a very isolating activity. You might as well be in solitary confinement. It is just you and your computer, and a few of your closest buddies from CNBC who are talking to you all day long. You are concentrating on your charts, on your Level II stock box, on every detail. And at the same time, you are watching the dialogue in the chat room. You know these people. You are with the same people day in and day out. Every morning you say hello to them and crack a few jokes. Every day when the market closes you stand around the cyber water cooler and swap stories. These are your pals and colleagues, these are people like you.

When they start getting into trades and making big point gains, you are happy for them. But if they are just like you, shouldn't you be making the same gains? Well, if one of them is making a big gain, you can stay unemotional and detached. But if 10 or 20 people are saying they are making big bucks on a number of trades, and you start looking at your own performance and feeling it is deficient, sooner or later you will start feeling resentful. When enough resentment builds up, you need to do something! You're as good as any of these folks—maybe not better, but certainly as good—so how can they be making big bucks and you're making piddling profits?

The answer is that they are getting into breakouts, so the solution is simple—join them next time. And you do. And maybe you are successful. But that just builds up your confidence. Well, I knew I was as good as my pals. I can do this. I'll just get in the next breakout, too. And you do. And you lose. And you lose big. What did you forget? You forgot that there was a reason for writing the rule for yourself that said you were committed to not entering breakouts unless they followed a tight consolidation period. You set that rule because you used to enter those trades all the time, and for every ten dollars you made, you lost fifty dollars. You consistently lost money on those trades. You stink at those trades. But, you thought, "This time will be different."

You are thinking now that this can't happen to you. That you are not so influenced by group behavior. Picture this. You work in a corporation with a bunch of guys or gals that you've known since you graduated college. Good people, but real party people. You are all making about the same amount of money and you are all happy for your friendship. You really don't want to be fast tracked up the corporate ladder—too much responsibility. You would rather have the extra time to spend in your personal life. You are content until, one by one, each of your buddies starts getting promoted. Nice raises. More responsibility. Lots of parties toasting their success. It was great when it happened to the first one. You and the rest of your pals joked about how that one wouldn't be able to hang with the old gang anymore. No jealousy here. You have what you want—free time and lots of friends to share it with. But when more and more of your friends start getting promoted and its just you that hasn't, you don't feel so good anymore. You could understand if they were better than you but they are just like you. All of a sudden, your precious free time doesn't seem like such a wonderful commodity. You are angry, and resentful. You want your opportunity, your share. You are very emotionally charged and are feeling pretty resentful.

And this is exactly what happens and exactly how you feel when all of your trading chat room buddies are making the big bucks on the risky trades, and you are standing on the sidelines. If you aren't careful, disciplined, and rigid about following you own rules, you can easily start jumping into trades that are contrary to your best judgment and your best interest. I can guarantee that if you do that, you will start losing money. So observe yourself, and if you ever find yourself jumping into a trade that is not on your list of acceptable trading strategies, stop trading immediately. Sit down. Think. Reflect. Figure out why you did it and put some system in place to change your own behavior.

the fish that got away

Be careful about where you place your focus. If you focus backward, you will hurt yourself badly. On any given day, some stock will take off and soar almost to the moon. Sometimes, you might have heard the news before market but decided not to enter because it had already gapped up 5 percent. How much higher could it go? Well, sometimes it goes a lot higher, and you are sitting on the sidelines. You didn't have an acceptable entry set-up that would have let you take that trade, so not entering the trade was a good thing because it followed your own established strategies. However, when the stock goes up an additional 10 percent and you are sitting on the sidelines, it is still hard to feel good about it. This is just another form of latent greed.

Oh, If I Had Only Caught the Latest Run-Up in the Nasdaq! Or in the Biotechs! Or in the Internets! Or in "anything"! You can count on experiencing this foray into the land of greed. Let's say you were demo trading while the Nasdaq went up 30 percent. Darn. If only it was real money. You missed what was rightly yours, or so your mind tells you. So you decide that you are going to get it now, even if the market may be ready for a reversal. You want your money and you want it now!

Yes, this is the hidden variety of greed, the kind that doesn't explode. It just festers, feels uncomfortable, feels like a mild stomachache. Beware. Latent greed leads to sloppy trading. Somewhere deep inside you start telling yourself, "Maybe my rules are too rigid; maybe they don't allow room for these exciting opportunities." That is your inside's way of tricking you to trade outside your well thought out trading strategies.

You cannot avoid latent greed. All you can do is have a system for avoiding its devastating effects. Make yourself a guideline that says you can never change, add, or remove one of your trading strategies without following a rigorous protocol. That protocol could take several forms. One possibility is *never* changing a strategy without first discussing it after hours with some trading colleague whose opinion you respect. Discuss all pros and cons. Discuss why you wrote the original strategy and explain what has changed that makes that original strategy worthy of change. Be sure you pick a trading colleague that you are not able to con. Prove your point *before* you ever trade with a new strategy or before you ever remove or change a strategy.

Another possibility is to demo trade your new strategy for at least five trading sessions before you implement it real time. Have a required demo success rate that is very rigorous, and never, ever adopt it for real-time trading until you have met or exceeded that required success rate.

Set up systems that prevent you from sabotaging yourself. None of us is beyond being influenced by latent greed, so plan for it to rear its ugly head and be prepared to avoid its negative influences.

cost of trading

There is an old adage that it costs money to make money. So, with day trading, there are some start-up costs you should anticipate.

getting started: the start-up cost
The tools listed below are what you need to get started to be close to maximum efficiency as a part-time trader. Reality is that a part-time trader needs the same hardware as a full-time trader.

SureStart > *Suggested Start-Up Equipment and Services*

Trading computer with 21-inch monitor (800 MHz Pentium III & 256 RAM)	$2,500.00
Second trading monitor, 17 inch (minimum)	$ 300.00

32 MB Millennium G400 Matrox dual monitor card	$ 250.00
A dedicated phone line for 56K modem, including ISP	$ 100.00
Training and books	$1,250.00
Total start-up cost	$4,400.00

Start-up costs do not include printer, furniture, etc. Your start-up costs may be lower depending upon your existing equipment or services. For those of you who will be doing fewer than 50 round-trip trades per month or those of you who want to minimize your initial investment in equipment, please refer to "Minimum Start-up Equipment and Services."

Minimum Start-Up Equipment and Services
(If you already own a computer with a minimum of a 266 Pentium processor with 128 megs of RAM, and a 17-inch monitor, that will be okay to start.)

Trading computer with 19-inch monitor	
(500 MHz Celeron & 256 RAM & v.90 modem) (Includes internal V.90 modem)	$1,500.00
Books	$ 200.00
Training (You will use all the free on-line training that is available to you.)	$ -0-
Total start-up cost	$1,700.00

ongoing trading cost
With the suggested start-up equipment and services there will also be data access and service fees:

Data and service fees	$100.00/month

Once you start making a minimum number of trades, usually 50 or more round-trip trades, there is no monthly charge for the software.

However, during your simulation trading you will be charged this fee because you will not be live trading.

Trading room	$100.00–250.00/month
Dedicated phone line, 56K and ISP service	$50.00/month
Total monthly ongoing expenses (during your training on live simulation software)	$250.00–400.00/month
Total monthly ongoing expenses upon live trading	$150.00–300.00/month

We are assuming 50 tickets or 25 round trips per month with no monthly data or service fees. This estimate does not include commissions.

With the minimum start-up equipment and services, we can forgo the data access and service fees:

Data and service fees	$-0-

There are no fees here because you are using less sophisticated trading programs such as CyBerX or E*Trade *and* you will execute your simulation trades on those services that are offered without charge.

Trading room	$-0-

You are using trading rooms that are available without cost. However, remember that you will be saturated with hype, so use caution when you participate in these free rooms.

ISP (no dedicated phone line)	$20.00/month
Total monthly ongoing expenses	$20.00/month

expenditures prior to live trading

We are assuming that you will not be making any live trades for at least the first three months during your learning phase. You will be earning no income from trading and you will not have the data and service fees waived because you did not live trade a minimum number of trades. So prior to actually trading live, you will have the following expenses:

With Suggested Start-Up Equipment and Services

Start-up cost	$4,400.00
Ongoing expenses enabling you to simulation trade live for 2 months ($250.00 × 2)–($400.00 × 2)	$500.00 – $800.00
Total expenditures prior to live trading	$4,900.00–5,200.00

With Minimum Start-Up Equipment and Services

Start-up cost	$1,700.00
Ongoing expenses ($20 × 3)	60.00
Total expenses prior to live trading	$1,760.00

summary for the part-time trader

As you can see, there is a wide range of costs and ongoing fees depending upon whether you are running at maximum efficiency or you are using minimum start-up equipment and services. You have to decide what you need based on what type of part-time trader you plan to be and what trading strategies you will be using. Reading through this book will help you arrive at that answer. As professional traders, we definitely recommend that you at least select a brokerage service that furnishes you with Level II quotes, even if you decide to go the minimum route. Depending on how much you trade and what brokerage firm you use, you may be able to get Level II quotes free or for no more than $100.00 per month. The biggest downside with the lowest cost plans are that you will have fewer charts and analytical tools available. Therefore, your entry and exit points may not be as well timed as they could be if you were using all the suggested equipment and services.

funding a trading account

We cannot tell you how much money you need in your part-time trading account. What we can tell you is that you must use only your discretionary funds for trading. Trading funds, if lost, should not alter your lifestyle or be a permanent emotional scar in your life.

As a basis for funding an account, we will review the possible returns and risks associated with different funding amounts for short-term momentum trading and the minimal funding aspects for consolidation-breakout trades.

short-term momentum trading

The following scenarios theoretically will generate the same amount of income, but read them carefully to understand the emotional difference in the two scenarios.

Trading Conservatively
This trader has $50,000 capital in a trading account and $100,000 buying power through margin. One profitable trade per day of 1,000 shares, at one-quarter point gain is $250 or approximately $210 after commissions. If you did this consistently for 20 days a month, you would have income of $4,200 per month or $50,400 for the year, less other noncommission expenses.

If you were able to do two one-quarter point profitable trades per day, at 1,000 shares, you would be earning approximately $420 per day, $8,400 per month or $100,800 per year, less other noncommission expenses.

The basis for grossing $250 or $500 per day will be trading a slow-moving, high-volume, liquid stock such as CSCO. Each trade would consist of 1,000 shares, and you are exiting at one-quarter profit.

At the time of this writing, CSCO is trading at $74/share.

Dangers of Trading with Less Capital
This trader has $20,000 capital in trading account, and $40,000 buying power through margin.

One profitable trade per day of 500 shares, at one-half point gain is $250 or approximately $210 after commissions or two one-half point profitable trades at 500 shares is $420 after commissions. You would have the same monthly and yearly income as in "Trading Conservatively" with CSCO.

The basis for grossing $250 or $500 per day in this scenario will be trading a fast-moving stock that is in the news, that has had an analyst upgrade, and that has had an outstanding earnings report. The trading of a stock such as this may be riskier than trading CSCO as the stock in the news may be more volatile, faster moving, and may have wider spreads and less liquidity than CSCO.

Be forewarned: momentum trading for one-half point gain is usually a greater risk than trading for one-quarter point gain in a more conservative, high-volume stock. The chances of overall success are much more in your favor with $50,000 in trading capital than with $20,000 in trading capital because with the higher capitalized account you can trade more shares of less-risky stocks, taking smaller, more-assured profits.

One-quarter or one-half point per day sounds easy. Don't forget, however, that there are inevitably days of losses along with days of higher profitability. The key to your success as a part-time trader will depend on your skills, your discipline, and your ability to take a predetermined stop loss.

Trading with Funds in Excess of $50,000, with Buying Power in Excess of $100,000
Obviously, once you have reached a level of consistent profitability with smaller share lots in various types of trades, having more capital will be very beneficial to you in booking larger dollar profits. Now, instead of trading 1,000 shares of CSCO, you could trade 2,000 shares and, with a profitable trade, double your dollar profit versus trading with 1,000 shares. Higher-priced conservative stocks are now open to you for trading such as INTC, presently trading at $78, and MSFT, presently trading at $93.

Additionally, as your ability to trade improves, you will be able to trade more than one stock at a time in 1,000 share lots. This will add flexibility to your trading. Depending upon the capital you have, there will be different trading strategies open to you.

Importance of Adequate Trading Capital

Having enough capital to trade is important. Having insufficient capital will cause you to trade differently than you might trade if you had adequate capital. If you are trading with $20,000 in capital, you may be trading higher-risk stocks and holding them longer in an attempt to get the same profits that you could earn if you were working with $50,000 in capital. Nevertheless, you can succeed if you educate yourself properly, have patience, discipline, and apply stop losses.

Some of you will have limited capital. If that is the case, you can search for lower-priced stocks that are on the move because of news, earnings reports or analyst upgrades. Another option is trading some stocks for swing or position trades, holding them for one or more days.

If you wish to be conservative with your $20,000, there are some limitations in gains achievable. You could buy 500 shares of CSCO at today's current price. You could hold for a one-quarter point gain and sell. Your gross profit would be $125 or approximately $85 after commissions.

You can build your portfolio with less capital, but it will be more difficult as you are making fewer profits to offset losses, which will occur no matter how good you are at trading. You could also hold your 500 shares longer, risking a one-quarter point profit for a higher profit of three-eighths point or even one-half point. This is harder to do when you are new at trading, but with experience you can aim for higher profits. Over time, you will have a better sense of when to get out, when to hold through a slight pull back (known as a wiggle), and how to get out quickly when a real reversal in price starts.

The real difficulty of having an undercapitalized account is getting through the learning curve with enough capital remaining to trade effectively.

consolidation-breakout trading strategy

There is a favorable method of trading with minimal capital. We will speak of consolidation-breakout plays here as if we were going long.

However, as discussed in our "Consolidation-Breakout Trading Strategy" in Chapter 5, breakout plays can also be to the down side or can go short. The profits and stop losses are all similarly applicable.

With consolidation-breakout trading your risk versus reward is in favor of reward. The upside potential on a stock consolidating after an upward move would normally be greater than the one-quarter or a one-half point profit that you would be happy to take in a short-term momentum trade. In addition we are trading consolidation-breakout plays in the direction of the daily trend of the stock, which is another factor leading to a more successful trade. Quite often consolidation-breakout plays will run a point or two.

For those of you with less capital, trading consolidation-breakout plays could be more favorable for you because you are more likely, even in a short-run breakout, to cover your commission costs even with only 100 or 200 shares. For example: If you have $10,000 in trading capital, your margin account would be $20,000, or $20,000 available for trading. If you are trading a $100 stock, 100 shares will use $10,000 of those funds. If you enter the breakout as we suggest and it makes a one-half point gain before it weakens, you will exit with a one-half point gain of $50, which is approximately $10 net after commissions. With 200 shares, at one-half point profit, you net $60 after commissions. With consolidation breakouts, your point gain will usually exceed one-half point profit on a $100 stock, so your profits will increase accordingly.

Now we have to repeat our advice regarding stops, because this is where money management comes into play. You must faithfully keep your stops. When you entered this consolidation, as we suggested in our consolidation-breakout trading strategy, you set your stop immediately below the lower range of the consolidation. By keeping this stop, you can have a very small stop loss.

Because you have a significant upside potential with consolidation-breakout plays and a narrow stop loss, your reward versus risk is very favorable. From a capitalization standpoint you can trade with less capital because your odds of earning more profit per trade are usually greater and less risky.

Due to the conservative nature of the consolidation-breakout strategy and your minimal stop losses, you can also trade stocks that have a wider intraday trading range compared to a more conservative stock such as CSCO. In other words, you can trade stocks that are more volatile when they are in a consolidation pattern. This will improve your chances for making a larger profit when such stocks break out of their consolidation.

If you are limited to a $10,000 trading account, you can build up your trading account in a safe and conservative manner with careful attention to consolidation-breakout trades and the utmost diligence to your stop losses.

Is $10,000 the minimum that you can start with to build up an account? We let you be the judge of that. It certainly will be harder but not impossible to start with less. A good way for you to determine this without spending any money is to play consolidation-breakout trades using the delayed-data simulator. See how you do in simulation trading starting off with whatever capital you can have available for trading. Remember, with the free simulator, you do not have the S&P and Nasdaq futures to aid you in trading.

Trading Capital for Consolidation-Breakout Trades

The amount of capital necessary to trade breakout plays is not as critical as with short-term momentum trades. Take profits when the stock weakens or hits your trailing stop. Do not stay in a trade after your stop is hit. If you do, this is a sign that you are trading with an underfunded account, and you are likely to fail. Follow the strategy carefully to set your entry and exit points. Don't stay in the trade based on hope.

Your learning curve here is very important. However, we believe there is a shorter learning curve here than with short-term momentum trades. Trading consolidation breakouts is more mechanical, and you will recognize the patterns sooner than with short-term momentum trading. Also, there are good conservative calls coming from trading rooms that can help you set your entry and exit prices.

So, to preserve your trading capital and to get yourself through the learning curve, practice on a simulator with live data, then make your move to trading live. Your chances of making it through the learning curve are immensely improved with this approach.

your trading account and your learning curve

We are going to give you two examples of a part-time trader starting off with a trading account funded with $50,000. Remember, we do not envision anyone quitting full-time employment to trade with $50,000 in capital. Be sure you are a very successful part-time trader before you even consider quitting any income-producing job.

Our examples of Trader I and Trader II in the learning curve are based on their entry into trading as short-term momentum traders. However, the same overall scenarios apply to those who start their trading with consolidation breakouts.

part-time trader I (we hope this is not you)

After start-up expenses, you have $50,000 remaining to trade with. You also have a 100 percent margin account so your buying power is $100,000 worth of stock.

You start trading live by buying 1,000 shares of CSCO. A one-quarter point profit would gross you $250 or approximately $210 after commissions. Not bad! In theory, you could go on and build a nice nest egg with your $50,000 by making a one-quarter point profit each day. Sound easy? Well, it doesn't really work that way.

Time to face reality: this just isn't going to happen. Most likely, the first thing that will occur is that you will start trading live before three months of simulation trading is completed. Not that three months is any magic number, but it is certainly the minimum time to allocate to becoming somewhat educated and profitable at simulation trading. This is particularly true as a part-time trader. If you trade live before three months pass, you will probably be trading ahead of your learning curve. That is, before you are sufficiently educated, before you have had enough practice at routing your orders, and before you have had enough experience at simulation trading. Consequently, you will endure some immediate losses. If the history of what has happened to other traders repeats itself, and we know no reason why it would be any different with you, you will experience some large losses due to a failure to take stop losses. In addition to not taking stop losses, you are also likely to develop shaky hands and poor judgment from the stress of entering your first live trades.

In this example—in which you are trading at your maximum margin and experiencing losses, some of which are probably big because you did not take your *stop losses*—you will have less capital to trade as each day goes by. To make matters worse, CSCO is now trading at $74 per share, up from $60. Now you can't trade as many shares because of your dwindling capital account and the increase in the price of CSCO. With fewer shares, you make less profit on each one-quarter point scalp. Guess what happens next? You start hoping for a bigger profit on the shares that you are trading, contrary to your low-risk strategy. You don't take the profits when they are there at one-quarter point. Instead, you wait and hope for more. The stock turns, and you get out with less than a one-quarter point profit or even with a loss. As your capital diminishes, you are more prone to violate your stop loss commitment. Now you say to yourself, "Instead of taking my loss at one-eighth, I will hold it a little longer—maybe allow my loss at one-quarter—because I know it will turn around at that point." Guess what? It doesn't have to. You take another loss.

You have been watching the trading room to learn, to be educated by the host and by the actions of other traders. You have seen experienced traders posting profits from trading the host's calls, which are usually volatile, fast-moving stocks with wide spreads. You think that if they can do it, you can too. You jump into one of these calls. Wow! In and out, with twice the profit you were aiming for with your one-quarter point or $250 target per trade. You try this again. The host makes the next call. You are in long, and the stock has already moved up three-quarters of a point in less than a minute. You are licking your chops, seeing easy profits. What's happening? Something is going wrong! It's now going down. A panic, reversal sell-off has begun. Everyone is selling. Ever try to get out of a stock when everyone else has the same idea? It is almost impossible to get out until the selling abates. Finally, you sell. You have just taken a one-point loss on 1,000 shares of a $16.00 stock. You just loss $1,000 and are probably lucky that you did not lose more. It takes experience not to be greedy! It takes skill to get out of a fast-moving stock with a profit. It takes experience to see a reversal coming and use the proper routing techniques to get out and avoid a loss.

You have now experienced the ultimate stop loss: you do not have enough capital to trade. You are done as a trader. You have used all your discretionary capital, so please do not look to your nondiscretionary capital to continue your trading. We do not want you to be this type of trader. We will now show you how to become a successful trader.

part-time trader II (the trader you will be)

You have the same $50,000 capital and $100,000 buying power as Trader I, and you will be trading the same stock, CSCO, but your approach to trading will be much different. You are going to treat trading as a part-time business. You will allow time to turn a profit, and you are going to prepare yourself carefully and not take unwarranted risks.

Because you are part-time, you are not depending on the income that you will earn from trading. You will be patient. You are going to become educated and skilled before you start trading. You are going to avoid the temptation to trade live in the first three months and will wait longer if you're not consistently profitable in simulation trading. You will be watching an educationally oriented trading room. You will continue to read. You will not listen to hype. You will simulation trade day after day using simple analytical tools for entries, such as going long on the one-minute stochastic bounce from the zero band. You will increase your chance of success by going long only in up-trending markets. Very important to your trading success: you must carefully watch the daily and intraday support and resistance levels on the stock you are trading. In addition, be sure that the S&P futures, Nasdaq futures and the Nasdaq 100 composite index are moving in the same direction as the trade you are ready to enter. Also, carefully observe the support and resistance levels on these futures and indices as they will often be places the market tends to slow or reverse.

Additionally, you will use this time to understand how shorting works. You will practice shorting using the same analytical tools as going long. To keep your probabilities of success high, you will short only on down-trending market days. You will approach all your simulation trades with the same seriousness you would if they were live trades. You will use the same care, analysis, and tight stop loss discipline as you would if you were trading your own hard-earned money. You will take each loss and gain very seriously, even if it is just a paper gain or loss.

When you begin simulation trading, you will keep a journal of your trades. You will write down why you entered a trade, and why it was or wasn't successful based on your parameters for entry. By keeping this journal faithfully, you begin to see what works and what doesn't. You begin to recognize your repetitive mistakes, enabling you to avoid them in the future. We know of many traders, including ourselves, who didn't keep a journal until things started to turn negative. Keeping a journal and reviewing it is one of the keys to becoming a successful part-time trader.

Now that you have simulation traded for approximately three months and are being consistently profitable, you are going to begin live trading. If three months have passed and you still do not feel confident, continue simulation trading until you do or make the decision that trading may not be for you.

You are not going to start live trading using your full buying power. What you are going to do is start off with a small number of shares, say 100, or a maximum of 200. Trading live puts you on a different emotional level. By this time, you have read the book, *The Disciplined Trader*, several times over. This book will help you understand how your emotions can work against you in trading and will give suggestions for remedying this.

When you trade your first 100 or 200 shares live, your hands might shake and your heartbeat will most certainly accelerate. After a few trades, whether successful or not, you will be over the jitters.

Despite the jitters, you will be making your first trades with confidence, just like your simulation trading. You will be taking profits the same way as you did in simulation trading at one-quarter point gains. When you first start live trading, trading 100 to 200 shares, it is important to keep your profit goals focused on the point gain, not the dollar gain. If you do not, you may shift away from your successful trading strategy of taking small profits with less risk and start aiming for bigger profits with more risk. Do not do this. This is not the way to start trading live.

What follows is an example of how and why your trading strategy might change from simulation trading to live trading with $100,000 in buying power:

> Simulation Trading: 1,000 shares at one-quarter-point profit is approximately $210 after commissions.
>
> Live Trading: 200 shares at one-quarter-point profit is approximately a little more than break even after commissions.

To make up the dollar amount when trading smaller shares, you decide to let your profits run longer, say to one point, contrary to your simulation trading strategy of booking small point profits. You hope this will give you approximately $160.00 in profit after commissions. That's OK if the market (as well as your stock) are trending higher, but in the real world that just doesn't happen all the time. In a slow-moving stock like CSCO, there are not going to be too many straight runs of a full point. A stock like CSCO is more likely to gain a one-quarter, three-eighth, or even a one-half point. Therefore, you may end up holding your position too long and not taking the smaller one-quarter-point profit before you can exit the trade. Then you end up having a loss. The saying is: "Exit when you can, not when you have to."

The key to transitioning to live trading is to continue trading with the same strategy you used in simulation trading regardless of the immediate dollar profit or loss. The goal in moving from simulation trading to live trading is to continue trading successfully.

To build your confidence, base your initial live trades on small one-quarter-point moves as you did in simulation trading. You may not make much money to start, but you need to book winning trades, however small, to build your confidence. Do this despite showing a small loss on your profit-and-loss statement after commissions. Better to lose a little here in the learning curve, than to risk losing your confidence. This is not the time to be thinking big profits. Your time for trading larger share lots will come soon enough. Be patient.

It is important to treat your 100 or 200 share size with the same stop loss as you would if you were trading 1,000 shares. Stop losses are your key to success as they preserve your capital. Do not say to yourself, "It's only 200 shares, I can let my loss go a little further, and it will come back." Do *not* do this! If you get into this habit with 200 shares, do you think you will change with 1,000 shares? You won't!

As you feel comfortable with your ability to trade, move up in share size. Your profits will increase on your winning trades because of the increase in share size. You will learn the rhythm of one stock, in this example, CSCO. You will know when to let your profits run, so instead of taking only a one-quarter-point profit you may get three-eighths-point profit or even a one-half. Soon, while increasing your profits on trades and minimizing your losses due to your discipline in taking stop losses, your weekly and monthly profit-and-loss statements will be positive and growing.

How long before this happens? From our experience and from hearing from other full-time traders, three months to a year is a reasonable estimate of the time it will take you to trade profitably on a consistent basis. Because you will be starting on a part-time basis, you should expect this process to take a minimum of six months to a year. Once you get to this level with conservative stocks and the simplest of charting analyses, you will be able to expand with confidence into other trading strategies and more volatile stocks.

Following the example of Trader II, you may be wondering how much capital you have left before you become a consistently profitable trader. We do not have the answer nor does anyone else. As in any business during the start-up phase, there is a learning curve before you become profitable. This means losses. However, we are sure of two things:

1. If you take predetermined stop losses, your losses will significantly decrease.

2. If you take the patient conservative approach to trading as Trader II did, your chances of succeeding are far greater than if you follow the reckless path taken by Trader I.

how much capital is enough to survive the learning curve?

We have been asked this question many times over: "What amount of capitalization is required to cover losses that will occur during the learning curve so that I will still have enough capital to trade once I become consistently profitable?"

The answer is dependent on each individual's ability to learn, execute orders, apply discipline and most importantly, to hold predetermined stop losses.

If you follow the path of Trader I, there is no limit to your losses, other than the total of your trading account. You will never become a successful trader.

Give Yourself Plenty of Leeway

We start off by suggesting what you might set aside for losses during the learning period. The figure is high: $25,000. You may groan and say, "That is all that I have to invest." Others will say, "I just barely have $10,000 to invest." As a start, we feel that we have to give you just about the worst-case scenario of what it might take in terms of dollars before you become profitable.

On the brighter side, your learning period really need not be so expensive if you follow some sound advise. Remember, just as in school, some of you will learn quicker than others, and it is no different here. So here are our suggestions:

Get educated: books, courses, trading rooms, other traders, etc.

Use the free delayed-data simulation software available until you know it thoroughly and have practiced your trading strategies until you are very successful as a simulation trader.

When you have opened your account, practice all your trading skills and strategies on a simulator using live data, including the use of the S&P and Nasdaq futures data.

Pick a trading strategy that is successful for you. This will depend on how much trading capital you have and will certainly depend on your trading skills and your level of discipline. We would cautiously say that beginning your trading career with consolidation-breakout trades would be less risky than starting with short-term momentum trading.

Keep your stop losses!

A lot of this is repetitive. We know that. We want this to sink in. We want you to succeed!

Real Life for Many
If possible, you may wish to start your account at $25,000 more than what you will need to trade once you are consistently trading profitably. If you need at least $25,000 to trade on an ongoing basis, you should fund your account with $50,000. You are allowing yourself losses of $25,000 until you trade profitably. If you take Trader II's approach to trading, your losses should be significantly smaller and you will have more capital to build your equity once you are trading profitably.

Some of you will or should start with $10,000 as an allocation of funds to use during the learning period. Others will start trading with $10,000 in their trading account and will be limited to how much they can afford to run their balance down during the learning period by their broker's minimum balance requirement.

As with the stop loss in your trades, you will determine your learning-period stop loss in advance of starting to trade live. If you reach your learning-period stop loss, stop trading and accept the fact that you are not suited for trading. Move on with your life.

For some of you, losing $25,000 during the beginning of live trading will be a reality no matter how diligently you study, practice, or simulation trade. Some reasons for this are explained in the book, *The Disciplined Trader*. To take losses beyond $25,000 is your decision. However, please give this a lot of serious thought. From our experience and from our observation of others, we certainly would not suggest continuing if you have exceeded this size loss.

You may have heard that many traders lose more than $100,000 learning to trade. This is a frightening statistic, but most of these traders did not have the educational resources that you have available to you and the opportunity to simulation trade. Many traders started trading with large lot sizes—2,000 to 5,000 shares. Additionally, they started their trading careers trading very volatile, fast-moving stocks with wide spreads. With a conservative approach to trading, holding to small losses and the ability to simulation trade, you should be able to tell if you have what it takes to be successful long before you lose $25,000. You must set yourself a boundary and not go beyond it. This applies to you regardless of what amount of capital is in your trading account.

Some of you will be celebrating. You have taken the right path as Trader II did. You have followed our suggestions. You have conserved your capital by taking small losses on your losing trades. You consistently took your predetermined stop loss. You did not lose $25,000 of capital while learning how to trade. You will be a successful part-time trader. Congratulations!

chapter 7

nuts and bolts

computers and monitors

We place our **SureStart** designation on a system in this category, but not on a particular vendor. There are many vendors that can provide products and services that are comparable in price and quality to the one we chose. Additionally, we assume that many of you have your own favorite suppliers, and it is very easy to check on the Web for quotes on whatever you wish to purchase. We talk about one vendor's products so we can be consistent in the comparative pricing of different levels of computer systems and monitors.

We have elected to put computers and monitors in the same section because purchasing them together is more cost effective. The information we provide is very basic. We site examples primarily from one vendor, Dell.

We strongly suggest that you have one computer dedicated to your trading. Use it for nothing else. This will ensure maximum performance and reliability for your trading. We know that not everyone will have this luxury, but if you can, do so.

If you already have a computer, your present equipment may be adequate to start trading with, particularly as a part-time trader. As a matter of fact, one of us did just that and has not yet felt the need to upgrade.

RAM or SDRAM (Synchronous Dynamic Random Access Memory) is probably the most critical component of your computer. RAM enables a system to run applications and temporarily store data being used by your system. With software like CyBerTrader and RealTick, there can be a tremendous amount of data flowing into your computer with many windows open and all sorts of data being sorted and processed in these open windows. The more RAM you have, the smoother everything will run.

We do not suggest trying to view data from CyBerTrader or RealTick on anything less than a 19-inch monitor. There is just too much to see, and not enough viewable area to see it all if the monitor is any smaller. All monitors considered are color monitors. Although it is not in our **SureStart** suggestion, if you can afford it, we highly recommend going with two monitors connected to the same computer. There is just a lot of data to see, and it is much more viewable on two monitors than one. Connection to the Internet with a 56K modem will work; however, we suggest using an ISDN or DSL connection because it is likely that you will be transferring more data using the two monitors. Better yet is a 128K frame-relay line. We will provide more details on ISP connections later in this chapter.

All systems should be equipped, at minimum, with a 56K V.90 capable analog modem. Depending on Internet connection upgrades, internal modem changes can be made or external modems can be utilized.

Pricing does not include shipping and handling cost. Pricing is for comparison shopping within the same vendor's product range, in this case Dell Computer Corporation. Please note that prices are rounded off considerably, and we only list major components. For accurate and up-to-date comparison shopping, check on-line with Dell or other vendors for a detailed description of components and software that are included in the package you are considering.

minimum computer and monitor requirements

If you already own some equipment, it is okay to start with the following:

266–500 Pentium processor with 128 megs of RAM

19" monitor

Approximate Cost: $1,500

 800 MHz Pentium III processor with 256 megs of RAM

21" Trinitron 1600HS monitor

20.4 GB hard drive

Approximate cost $2,500

Product comparison name: Dell Dimension XPS T

flying high

If you have extra money to spend or just like being equipped with top-of-the-line equipment, consider these:

800 MHz Pentium III processor with 512 megs of RAM

Two (2) Trinitron 1600HS 21" monitors

MATROX G400 MAX 32 MB (Dual monitor video card)

20.4 GB hard drive at 7,200 rpm

Windows NT Workstation 4.0

Approximate cost: $5,000

Product comparison name: Dell Precision Work Station 220

For some other interesting hardware for traders, go to Dell's "Financial Trading" Web page.

just for fun

We thought we would let you know of some other items that are available:

Eizo Nanao 18" LCD flat panel LCD monitor

Comments from manufacturer: "Ideal LCD for financial institutions"

Approximate cost: $3,500

Available through Dell

NEC Technologies, Inc. 20" Flat Panel LCD Monitor

Approximate cost: $4,300

Available through Dell

other monitors

We have heard traders praise certain models of ViewSonic 21" monitors, namely the P810, P815 and P817. We have traded using these monitors during visits to other traders and have marveled at their clarity and definition. Other traders we know are very fond of their Sony monitors.

With computers and monitors there are a lot of choices. Do your homework. Here is a list of Web sites for the aforementioned vendors and some others with comparable products:

Compaq (www.compaq.com)

Dell Computer Corporation (www.dell.com)

Dell Computer Corporation, Financial Trading

Under "The Software You Use" go to Financial Trading. Find, "Dell Recommended Solutions For Financial Traders." Very interesting and worthy of your consideration. (www.dell.com/products/work stat/index.htm)

Gigabuys (Dell's outline store third party products) (www.giga buys.com)

Gateway (www.gateway.com)

ViewSonic (www.viewsonic.com)

NEC Technologies, Inc. (www.nec.com)

backup power supply and surge protectors

If you are in the middle of a fast-moving trade and the power goes down, what would you rather do: Call your broker and ask that he close out your trade (time: one to two minutes, which is a long time if you're scalping for a small profit); or continue on with battery power, knowing that you have 10 to 15 minutes to see how the trade is going and exit at the push of a button on your own computer. We will take the second choice, thank you!

With a battery backup system, often referred to as a UPS (uninterrupted power supply), you have the luxury of staying in your trade. Quite often, power outages are less than a minute. With backup power, you can hang in a little longer to gain more profit or exit immediately if a reversal starts. If, after a few minutes, your main power does not come back up, it would be wise to exit any scalp trade.

There are daily power losses to our homes and businesses that you normally don't notice. With some UPS systems, the software automatically stores the time and extent of the power loss sustained. It is amazing the number of times we experience these small power losses. Your trading software's performance can be affected by these small power losses.

Therefore, we highly recommend getting backup power to your trading computer. We have only dealt with one company in the past two-and-one-half years, and because the batteries and software have performed flawlessly during that time, we will give our **SureStart** designation to American Power Conversion.

SureStart ⟩ American Power Conversion has an excellent on-line site that allows you to enter information about your computer, monitor, and so forth into their Enterprise UPS Selector. All very simple. Their selector will tell you what UPS model you should purchase.

For each grouping of computer, monitor, printer, and modem, we installed the American Power Conversion Back-UPS Pro 650. This UPS might be overkill, but we would rather be over-prepared here. The UPS comes with software that not only tracks power fluctuations but also allows you to program a systematic shut down of all your open windows, programs, and your computer in case you are away at the time of a power outage. You can even delay the shut down for up to 30 minutes, depending on what you have connected to the system. The cost may seem high, but it is not, for your peace of mind.

Keep in mind that in order to protect your computer and monitor against damage from power surges, you need to make sure that anything connected into your computer is also plugged into the UPS, which also acts as a surge protector.

There are some other companies out there besides American Power Conversion, which seems to be the biggest. Check them out as well.

American Power Conversion (www.apcc.com)

Back-UPS Pro 650 (one for each computer/monitor configuration)

Approximate battery life: 3 years

Approximate cost: $379 each

Tripp Lite (www.tripplite.com)

Deltec Electronics (www.deltecpower.com)

Internet service

Your Internet connection involves many components and many choices that are not always as clear-cut as we would like. Information regarding connectivity comes from many sources. Your final choices for Internet Service Provider (ISP) and modem will be based on cost, reliability, and availability. Furthermore, your decisions may be limited by your existing phone lines and physical location. Depending on where you live and the type of Internet services available, the cost of different Internet connections will vary. A good thing to remember: Learn to trade cheap until you learn to trade well.

All the computers that we have suggested to you are capable of handling any of the Internet connections described below. For other than a 56K connection, you will need the type of modem or router required to handle that particular connection.

There are many subjective factors in picking the best connection including your trading volume, location, and budget. Our **SureStart** designation in this section is given based on those part-time traders who average upwards of four round-trip trades per day. Our **SureStart** designation is given to ISDN for its proven reliability. DSL, from a cost factor, may be the appropriate choice for those of you who can access this service.

methods of connecting to the Internet
The most desirable connection is listed last, not considering cost. Satellite connection is not considered here. If that is your only means to connect to the Internet, you will need to research that method independently.

> 56K analog
>
> Cable modem
>
> DSL
>
> Dedicated ISDN
>
> T-1 or Fractional T-1
>
> Frame-relay

Some traders and technicians may list DSL ahead of ISDN on this priority list because of DSL's speed and lower cost. However, we consider reliability to be a more important consideration. We do not want our connection dropping when we are about to exit a trade.

Services, promotions, and prices may change. Please use the information and pricing given only as a relative comparison of each type of service. Please check with ISPs for their most recent information on pricing and services available. Prices can vary greatly for the same service in different locations.

56K Analog Dial-In Access

> Connectivity: Up to 56Kbps (for comparison, think 40Kbps–46Kbps)
>
> Advantage: Broadly available and inexpensive
>
> Approximate set-up cost: None, assuming your computer has a modem

Approximate monthly fees for line services: $15–$20 (best to use a phone line dedicated to trading)

Approximate monthly fees for ISP service: $20.00

Approximate total monthly fees: $35–$40

Initially, 56K modems were developed using two different technologies, K56flex and K56×2. The new international standard for 56K data communications is known as v.90. 56 K modems let you connect to the Internet at the theoretical maximum speed of 56,000 kilobits per second (Kbps) or 56Kbps, 56 K for short. The Kbps are also thought of in terms of bandwidth or the amount of space that is available for data to flow into and out of your computer. More Kbps is essentially the same as more bandwidth. A definition for *bandwidth* given in a technical glossary: "This is a reflection of the size of the capacity of a given transmission channel. In digital transmission, bandwidth is described in bits per second."

In actual practice, 56K is not achievable. First, the 56K standards developed allow only maximum download speeds of 53K, and upload speeds of 33.6K. Download speeds are the transmission rate to your computer from the Internet and upload speeds are the transmission rate from your computer to the Internet. Secondly, connection speeds are highly dependent upon the condition of local phone lines.

With 56K the new international standard for high-speed modems of v.90 connection speeds will be up to 53Kbps. In testing and in practical use, v.90 in reality runs at speeds between 40 to 46Kbps. So when comparing a 56K Internet connection with other connections, remember to think in terms of these slower speeds.

If you are limited to a 56K modem connection to the Internet, you should seriously consider using two 56K lines with two computers. One line is used strictly for your trading computer and the other for viewing a trading room, news, and other Internet activities.

If you are using only one computer for trading with a 56K modem you are going to have to practice being conservative with the number of windows that you have open with software like CyBerTrader and RealTick. Certain windows such as the Level II window, charts, and particularly charts with graphic overlays and analytical tools, eat up a huge amount of bandwidth. It is very easy to bog down a computer with all the data that can come from CyBerTrader and RealTick. To ensure smooth, continued connectivity with a 56K connection, you should consider limiting yourself to running only one Level II window and no more than four graphs. You need to experiment to see just how much data you can take in before your system slows. Just when you feel you have the right set-up for your connection, guess what? You go to a fast-moving stock that eats up more bandwidth and may cause your computer to slow or even freeze. This will distort what is occurring in the stock you are watching.

The bottom line is that traders need huge amounts of bandwidth to accept the amount of data they receive from CyBerTrader or RealTick. So when looking at these Internet connection options, remember that more speed and reliability will be the key issues.

Cable Connection
If you are considering a cable connection to the Internet via cable TV network, an alternative to phone modems, consider the following:

Connectivity: Up to 2,800K download, and 128K upload.

Advantages: High speed, low cost, connection always on, unlimited access.

Approximate set-up cost: $100–$200, depending on your cable provider.

Approximate monthly fees ISP service: $35–$65, depending on your cable provider and whether you are currently receiving your television programming through cable. We have heard of some much higher rates in different parts of the country, so please check in your area for total monthly fees.

Approximate total monthly fees: $35–$65. Check with your local cable provider.

A cable modem is an external device that hooks up to your computer. Instead of getting an Internet connection through telephone wires, you get connected though a cable network (your TV cable). Yes, you can watch TV and access the Internet at the same time.

Cable connections use the high-bandwidth capabilities of cable TV lines with proprietary caching and replication technologies to overcome bottlenecks that are inherent in other types of Internet connections. Speeds can vary because of overall network traffic, your computer's performance and configuration, location and configuration of accessing server, and number of users. It is difficult to say what your final download speed may be, but it will probably be on par with DSL. Availability is not yet widespread.

DSL (Digital Subscriber Line)
This is new technology that provides a dedicated digital circuit between a residence or a business and a telephone company's central office, or switch, allowing high-speed data transmission over existing copper telephone lines. Consider the following features:

Connectivity: Up to 1500K download and 348K upload.

Advantage: Fast, connection always on, unlimited access.

Approximate set-up cost: $0–$400. Includes modem cost and PC configuration. Consult your local DSL provider for actual quotes and package plans which may reduce costs.

Approximate monthly fees for line services: $20–$30. With one-year contract or using current phone line. 1500K or 1.5Mbps downstream data with 384K upstream data transmission (about max. DSL service).

Approximate monthly fees for ISP services: $30–$200.

Approximate total monthly fees: $50–$200. Consult your DSL provider for actual quotes and package plans. Many different DSL promotional programs available are being advertised.

Your location from the central office must be no more than 17,500 feet from the central office measured in telephone cable feet, not direct line of sight. Additionally, your existing telephone line must be capable of carrying the DSL signal. As an example, on the West Coast, Pacific Bell states that "On average, approximately 65 percent of customers serviced by DSL-equipped central office will qualify."

We find it interesting that one phone company stated that if you are within 17,500 cable feet of the central office but your line does not qualify, that the phone company can clean your line for a $900.00 fee. So if you really want DSL badly enough, there appears to be ways to overcome some of the obstacles. Amortized over two years of trading, that $900.00 fee works out to be $37.50 per month.

The big disappointment for most of you will be not having DSL available to you. There are three key reasons: (1) The central office is not DSL equipped, (2) the distance from central office is too great, and (3) the existing lines do not qualify for DSL.

DSL is a generic name for digital subscriber line, so when you see other names such as ADSL, SDSL, HDSL, IDSL, please remember that these are different variations of DSL offering different products and rates of transmission. If you have a choice between ADSL and SDSL, choose SDSL. Upload and download speeds are the same with SDSL.

Some of you will have choices in DSL services offered, for instance: 385Kbps downstream with 128Kbps upstream, or 1.5Mbps downstream with 384Kbps upstream. As a trader you would want the second with the higher downstream rate so that the data inflow to your computer would be the least restricted.

Though there may be an issue of reliability as compared to ISDN, for those of you who cannot afford ISDN, you may wish to give DSL some serious consideration over 56K analog dial-in access.

SureStart ▷ *ISDN (Integrated Service Digital Network)*
This is a complete digital phone connection that maximizes the transmission capabilities of existing copper wires, allowing for the simultaneous transmission of voice and data. Digital signals offer faster speeds, clear signals and error-free transmissions. These are some of the features of ISDN:

Connectivity: Up to 128Kbps.

Advantages: Fast, reliable, available, and not dependent on distance from the central office.

Appproximate set-up cost: $0–$500. Includes modem. Many different type of packages available. Check for actual quotes.

Approximate monthly fees for line service: $50–$200. This varies with different phone companies and their associated service plans. Some are fixed. Others are billed by the minute after so many minutes of free usage. Check with your local phone company for quotes. If you happen to be on-line all day, your line rate probably will be closer to $200 per month.

Approximate monthly fees for ISP service: $20–$300/month.

Approximate total monthly Fees: $70–$500/month.

ISDN is very reliable and available in most areas. The distance to your main hub is not a factor as with DSL. ISDN has been around for 10 years and the bugs have been worked out. Also, if your ISDN connection should go down, you can switch to 56Kbps analog through the dial-up properties in your computer.

ISDN lines to your home or business come from your local phone company. The ISDN lines installed by the phone company come with two channels known as B channels. Each channel runs at 64Kbps. Your ISDN modem will combine these two B channels to give you a connection speed of 128Kbps.

Not all ISPs provide ISDN service at 128Kbps, so if ISDN is your choice of connectivity, check the ISP before signing up to see if it has the capability to handle two B channels at 64Kbps. Some only offer one at 64Kbps and have you believing that you are flying at 128Kbps.

As we found out, not all homes have the proper wiring from the "neighbor box," as the phone company calls it. Usually this box is surrounded by a cluster of homes and not far from any one home. In our case, our home was not wired to handle ISDN, which was determined by a visual inspection from the phone company. The catch was that we had to provide the access for the wiring and the proper conduit for it. This required having a trench dug along the phone company's right-of-way through two of our neighbor's back yards. Then we had to place conduit in the ground to the phone company's specifications connecting the two points. Also, we had to provide the string (line) for the phone company to pull their wire through the conduit. What some of us will go through for high-speed connectivity! We tell this story because it is real-life stuff!

If you are serious about trading, and it is within your budget, we strongly suggest the ISDN connection for your trading computer.

T-1, Fractional T-1 Lines, and Frame-Relay Connections
These types of Internet connections are very sophisticated and expensive. They provide you with maximum capacity to use all the trading data that is available from a provider such as CyBerTrader or RealTick.

Speeds can be up to 1.544Mbps or 15,440K. The key to these systems in addition to the speed of transmission is their reliability. Also, there is very little interference on fractional T-1 lines and frame-relay lines as compared to a 56K dial-up access.

With a fractional T-1 line you connect to the Internet on a dedicated line, and share a designated portion of the bandwidth for which you contracted. Thus, you are always guaranteed a certain amount of bandwidth. However, with a T-1 line you are still connected to the Internet and as such are prone to the difficulties sometimes suffered by the backbone providers in the system.

Access to a fractional T-1 line and frame-relay is accessible through your local phone company. Cost can vary because each local phone company will have different access rates and each T-1 provider will have different connectivity plans. Two of the big T-1 providers are UUNET/MCIWorldCom and Sprint.

Full T-1 lines cost from $800 to $1,200. These costs include the provider and the local phone company's service charges

An additional cost associated with a fractional T-1 line is a router card for your computer. The router card functions as the modem for your Internet connection. Prices vary from $1,000 to $2,000.

A frame-relay connection is not an Internet connection. It is a private dedicated connection using a high-speed frame-relay network.

There is no dialing or disconnect issues involved. You are not subjected to the slow downs and outages associated with the Internet. A frame-relay connection is point to point, with no sharing of your bandwidth. No sharing means no interference.

A frame-relay connection running at 64K is the minimum of the frame-relay lines available. CyBerCorp now recommends using a frame-relay connection running at a minimum of 128K. Excluding cost, this is the best way to trade. This is highly recommended by CyBerCorp's networks department.

Frame-relay connections can run from $1,000 to $1,500 per month in addition to the one-time cost of a router: $1,500–2,000.

When we first contracted our frame-relay line, we bought 34K of bandwidth with another 34K available as a burst when needed. The catch was that you were provided the 34K burst if it was available from the frame line you were using. In other words, you were borrowing someone else's bandwidth if they were not using it.

Guess what? It seems that when we needed the extra bandwidth, so did everybody else! After several experiences with this dilemma, we contracted for the full 64K and never had a problem since. If you are being sold bandwidth based on a burst of additional bandwidth, consider that it won't be there when you really need it.

If you have any interest in either of these types of Internet connections, we recommend that you contact sales representatives concerning these products. CyBerCorp only uses MCIWorldCom for frame-rely connections. You can contact CyBerCorp for the name and phone number of their MCIWorldCom representative.

You might also check to see if other brokerages are working exclusively with one company and then contact the sales representative that they recommend. The benefits are that these representatives know what type of service and hardware you will need to connect to the broker's servers. Additionally, they frequently offer package deals.

The CyBerCorp Web site has a very detailed section entitled, "How can I connect to CyBerBroker?" Of course, this discussion can be used to help you in connecting to any brokerage firm of your choosing. This section can be found under CyBerCenter. The CyBer-

Frame section would only be applicable to a connection to CyBer-Broker.

Backbone Connectivity
Because most of you will be using 56K DSL or ISDN services we will first discuss the basic property of all ISPs using these connections: backbone connectivity.

This is the major routing system for your Internet connections. This is what your ISP connects you to when you use the Internet. Listed below are the primary backbone systems in the order of preference of acceptability by traders and software technicians we have talked to. (There is probably just as much subjectivity here as anywhere else on the subject of Internet connections.)

UUNET Technologies (an MCI WorldCom company)

SPRINT Communications Company (owns or is affiliated with Earthlink)

PSINet, Inc.

Your ISP. Your ISP connects you to a backbone system. ISPs come in three tier levels:

Tier 1: Dial in to the ISP and you connect to the backbone connectivity.

Tier 2: Dial in to the ISP and they connect you to the backbone connectivity.

Tier 3: Dial in to a company other than a true ISP and they connect you to the backbone connectivity.

Ideally, you should have a Tier 1 ISP. However, a Tier 1 ISP may not be available for the service you want. UUNET also advertises in some areas as an ISP, and in this case would be a Tier 1 ISP. MCI WorldCom, which is an ISP, is linked to its own backbone UUNET.

Additionally, your ISP should be associated with more than one backbone, so if one system goes down, they can switch you over to another. Alternatively, if you have more than one ISP, which is a good idea for backing up your trading system, make sure the second ISP has a different backbone system.

How Do You Find the Right ISP Service? We are lucky here. The Internet site, Boardwatch, www.boardwatch.com, lists all the local ISPs in an area code and all the other in-state ISPs serving your area code. Best of all they list the backbone service of each ISP.

Once you have selected some possible ISP providers, you can go to the UUNET and PSINet Web sites and, using your area code, find out if there is a local hub telephone number serving your community. Do this to double check Boardwatch's information. If you find that the ISP you have selected does not have a local hub for the backbone service, you may be charged an hourly rate to connect.

Make sure your ISP has a local hub number for ISDN connections. If you chose one that didn't, and you wanted ISDN service, they would bill you an hourly rate for a toll-free connection to their closest ISDN service hub. This could get very costly.

When you contact an ISP to find out what backbone they are using and what Tier level they are, ask the following questions: "Are you a Tier 1 ISP provider?" Anyone remotely qualified should be able to answer this question for you. If the technician does not know what a Tier 1 ISP provider is, then ask, "Are you routing me directly to the backbone provider?" Then you can ask, "Who is your backbone provider?" If you are calling UUNET or Sprint, their answer should be Tier 1, because they offer ISP services and are the backbone providers.

You can go a step further once you locate an ISP that you think you will use. Ask them the question, "What is your address to the gateway?" This is a routing address that they use to travel the Internet. If you provide this information to the networking staff at CyBerCorp, they can tell you how good that connection to them may be. If it is not good, they will let you know that you should look for another ISP. Brokerage firms other than CyBerCorp's CyBerBroker, can hopefully perform this service for you also. You can also check with any trading room that you might use to see if they provide this service. It can save you money and time.

Once you get connected, you can "Ping"—or time—your connectivity speeds to your trading servers to see how well you are doing in transmission speeds. Until you get familiar with doing that, you can ask the tech or networking staff of your brokerage company to do that for you. Times are in milliseconds. They can tell you what would be considered a good range of transmission times. In general, if you are below 100 milliseconds, you can smile; that is an excellent connection speed.

Web Site Addresses for Information About Internet Connection

www.boardwatch.com

www.cybercorp.com/cybercenter/

www.home.com

www.mciworld.com

www.pacbell.com   Great stuff on ISDN and DSL

www.psi.net

www.rampnet.com   DSL glossary, types of DSL technology, and comparative matrix

www.sprint.com

www.uu.net

informational Web sites

Almost any Web site can be considered an educational Web site because you cannot help but learn something from each. However, some are more valuable than others. We give you a brief overview of these sites.

A word of caution: There is an enormous amount of information in just the few sites that we have suggested, so don't overload yourself. We suggest that you start your trading education by reading the books recommended in this guide, obtain hands-on training in the use of software such as CyBerTrader or RealTick and by enrolling in a trading room. The sites that follow will supplement those resources. Look for the **SureStart** mark for those to review first.

Sites are listed alphabetically. You can usually open subsections by going to the index on the home page and right clicking on the name.

www.allstocks.com

Allstocks.com is one of the most important Web sites you will find for important day-trading information. What is today's S&P Fair Value? Get real-time autorefreshing news free! What is happening with Globex futures after hours and what does that portend for the market opening? Charts. Stock picks. Mutual fund cash flows. As you get proficient in day trading, you will increasingly value the critical information that you will find on this site. It might not mean a lot to you the first month of trading, but keep this site bookmarked. It will definitely become a favorite.

World Markets

This Web page is part of Allstocks and can be accessed through their Web address but is worth a separate mention. Never underestimate the importance of foreign markets in influencing the U.S. market. This site shows continually updated charts on the performance of each of the key foreign markets. Find out what happened in Asia, what is happening in Europe. This can be critical during times of international crises.

www.bigeasyinvestor.com

SureStart Big Easy Investor is an incredible Web site. It is outstanding for charts, research, and scanning stock charts using your own criteria. Written by hedge-fund managers who found off-the-shelf programs too difficult to use, too expensive, and too slow. Particularly good for part-time traders who do swing trades because graphs are refreshed daily, shortly after the close of markets. You will have to download software from the Big Easy Investor Web site to use their charting services.

SureStart **www.cbs.marketwatch.com**
If you were to watch only one on-line financial Web site, this may be the one. It has so much information, it's easy to miss the really good stuff. So here is a guide. First, sign up for the free e-mail updates by looking for Have Your News Delivered and enter your e-mail address. It will give you several options that are available. Next, in the left-hand column, click on Headlines and bookmark this page. It has constantly refreshing market news: upgrades, downgrades, earnings, anything hot that could effect a stock will show up here. Just leave this window open all day and check for updates. Great if you day trade news plays. Finally, on the bottom of the home page you will see Investing Tools and Data and you can explore this section. There are some great free screening tools, a technical charting service, and calendars.

SureStart **www.clearstation.com**
Clear Station is one of the best free resources available on the Web. Take the time to explore all the possibilities of this site. Free sign up. You can get daily listing of stocks that triggered significant technical indicators—record price breakouts, bullish or bearish indicators, earnings surprises and upgrades. You can create your own Watch List of stocks, and this list will be analyzed daily for all breaking technical indications. Outstanding educational section with wonderful explanations on charting and key technical indicators. Sign up for e-mailed notifications of recommendations. Don't miss this one.

www.cyberinvest.com
CyberInvest.com is a good listing of educational Web sites and synopses of them. You can compare investing resources at hundreds of sites. The following are two of our favorites:

Market Monitors

Technical Analysis

www.dayinvestor.com

Dayinvestor.com provides stock alerts, rumors, a live ticker, and a chat room, as well as a trading community Web site. It provides free e-mail alerts and percentage gainers. Chart alerts are unique—what stocks are showing buy or sell signals, and what is the news that may be producing those signals. Worth a look.

www.e-analytics.com

This free site has a wealth of information that will be invaluable in your part-time trading. Even a section on insurance and retirement planning. Some very detailed information to help you understand options and futures. Two of our favorite sections for part-time traders are listed below:

Technical Analysis Resource Center

Tutorials on the key technical indicators: relative strength index, stochastics, moving averages, moving average convergence/divergence, on-balance volume, and more.

Glossaries

10 Financial Glossaries that contain just about everything an individual would need pertaining to all aspects of finance and investing.

SureStart > **http://finance.yahoo.com**
The Yahoo finance Web site is a must for anyone interested in day trading or investing. A wealth of information, including economic calendars, earnings calendars, quotes, technical analysis, statistics and indicators, and almost any topic concerning the equity markets. One of the best sources for stock news; if you see a stock moving and want to know what is happening, then there is a good chance you can find the answer here.

Join chats on stocks, join a stock club. Lots of information, some fact, some opinion. But in day trading, it is important to know what people think will happen because common beliefs often give rise to short-term momentum, both up and down.

We also like their charts for end-of-day analysis because they are very quick in coming up. You can look at many charts in a hurry.

www.earningswhispers.com

EarningsWhispers.com. Savvy day traders know that earnings season is a great time to make money, but you will do so much better if you have some idea of how the investment community is expecting a stock to perform. It is no longer good enough to meet analyst estimates. Companies are now expected to meet the whisper numbers: those expectations that set a new standard for a company's performance. This site gives you information on what whisper numbers are and how your favorite stocks are expected to perform this earnings season. Sign up for the free e-mail service to get the latest whisper number information sent to you.

www.financialweb.com

Financial Web is another gold mine. Lots of free information that is not readily available elsewhere. Good information on sector strength, including those important advance/decline statistics by sector. Explore this site when you have some time. It is well worth taking the time to get very familiar with its features.

> *StockTools*—This is one of the few sources for historical data. If you need to determine where a stock opened, closed, its high and low for any day in the past year, this site will provide that information easily.

www.ibbotson.com

This site is almost too good to be true. It contains hundreds of Web resources, including those you would otherwise never find. Good summary write-ups.

http://interactive.wsj.com

The *Wall Street Journal* Interactive Edition charges a small fee but it is extremely valuable. For only $59 a year, you can get access to two of the top news and editorial services on the Web: The *Wall Street Journal* and *Barron's Online*. These two publications not only report financial news, they often create it. Traders pay close attention to what these two publications say, and both positive and negative mention in either of these two publications is often associated with strong movement in the affected stocks.

www.investorwords.com

Investorwords is the biggest, best investing glossary on the Web. It contains a comprehensive glossary of investment terms. What is a stop? What is a strike price? What is a straddle? Excellent resource. Keep this one bookmarked.

www.ipomaven.com

IPO Maven. Lots of info on IPOs—listing of those recently filed (often an opportunity to look at related stocks—halo effect or the mother company which is doing the spin-off). Best IPOs. IPO earnings. Profile of IPOs—key business, competitors, and financials. Lots of good stuff here if IPOs are a strategy you choose to develop. Part-time traders, be extremely cautious with playing first day IPOs. Very risky, only for the experienced.

www.island.com

An absolute must visit. The Island book, as it is commonly called, functions in the same way a Level II screen does for Nasdaq stocks. See it to get the feel for the movement of a Nasdaq stock on a Level II screen. Additionally, many electronic brokerage companies do not provide the Island book on their software, so it is good to look at if you are only getting Level I quotes. By watching the Island book on this site you will see the "depth" or different price levels and quantities of a stock offered on the bid and ask on the Island ECN. This is essential for becoming a successful part-time trader.

www.lookaheadcharts.com

This site is fun and interesting, but don't count on it. They provide bar charts showing 20 days of a stock's history, and a five-day look-ahead period prediction. Look, investigate, consider it, but don't lose your money believing any site can accurately predict the future.

www.marketguide.com

A great site to look at daily. Listings of upgrades/downgrades, today's headlines, story stocks. Free research on individual stocks: quotes, news, price charts, earnings estimates, insider trading, institutional ownership. Filled with information that can help you plan your part-time trading day.

www.moneycrawler.com

A great site with many features. Two that we especially like are listed below:

> *Glossary*—"Welcome to the most comprehensive financial glossary on the web. This glossary is used by Yahoo!, Reuters, The New York Times, Wall Street City and many other popular sites."

> *Java Chat*—A variety of chat rooms, 10 total, ranging from the Blue Chip Room to The Rumor Mill.

www.mrci.com/lbr/index.htm

This is Linda Bradford Raschke's home page. It is filled with terrific articles on day trading, swing trading, tape reading, capturing trend days. See further description under "Trading-Room Web Sites," in Chapter 4.

www.mtrader.com

The Momentum Trader Web site is host to a high-quality day-trading chat room concentrating on playing gainers and dumpers (stocks that have gone down significantly usually on bad news). Ken Wolf is a respected professional trader and founder of The Momentum Trader. See further description under "Trading-Room Web Sites," in Chapter 4.

www.swingtrader.net

This is an excellent chat room for the part-time trader. Toni gives excellent calls on consolidation-breakout plays. Toni and Brandon give thorough, technically sound recommendations for swing plays, which are particularly good for part-timers who can't sit in front of their computer all day.

www.pristine.com

The Pristine Day Trader site has some of the best educational material on the Web, and it is free. Go to Free Area, click on Educational Reports, and sign up for some excellent reading. Free on-line course on "Using Nasdaq Level II," "Buying Stocks that Gap Open," and much more! Lots of excellent training for the new part-time trader. See further description under "Trading-Room Web Sites," in Chapter 4.

 ## www.quote.com

Bookmark this site. It is worth its weight in gold!

Charts . . . Live—Provides quotes on some key indices that show you what is happening in the market. $PREM.X, $TYX.X, $OEX, $TRIN are some. Many of these aren't available from even the most sophisticated brokerages, yet they are critical in determining when buy or sell programs may hit the market. This information is very complicated, so you might not be able to use it immediately, but it will become extremely important to you as your level of sophistication in trading increases.

www.rightline.net/calendar/index.html

This site has an excellent listing of expected dates for earnings reports, with key information about whether the earnings report is to be given before or after the bell. Never rely totally on this information. Even the best sources are sometimes off by a day, which could lead you to stay in a position during the time earnings are announced, and this is generally considered to be a high-risk strategy. If you are holding a position in any company going into earnings, check multiple sources for earnings dates or call the company directly to confirm.

www.sec.gov.com

This site is run by the U.S. Securities and Exchange Commission Office of Investor Education and Assistance. There are many good topics here for the starting part-time trader.

Learning About Investing . . . The Internet and On-line Trading—
Find out how to invest wisely and to avoid fraud on the Internet.
Also some good advice from SEC Chairman Arthur Levitt taken
from his speeches.

www.smartmoney.com

The SmartMoney Web site is an outstanding resource for important
news stories and a free SmartMoney newsletter that is full of important information. Set up a calendar, get free e-mail notifications of important events on a portfolio of stocks of your choosing, determine
which sectors are gaining and losing. Take your time investigating this
site—there is so much here that you don't want to miss!

Sector Tracker—What a beautiful way to see what sectors are
moving! Simple, clear, and concise.

Tools—Some interesting and imaginative ways of tracking the
market!

www.stockselector.com

StockSelector.com has some interesting, unique features: stocks that
are farthest below the analyst target price, the week's stocks with the
most significant change in analyst recommendations, the analysts'
most highly recommended stocks, and other important criteria. Buffett Track covers Warren Buffett's portfolio. A discussion board with a
separate board for every single stock. Some interesting stock screening tools.

www.stocksplits.net

StockSplits.net is a great educational site about playing stock splits.

The Manual—Preannouncement strategies; Presplit strategies;
when to get in, when to buy, when to get out. Remember, this is
someone's opinion. Any strategy can work one month and fail
miserably the next. Learn the general approach here, but remember to watch market conditions!

Splits Calendar—All the information you need regarding announced stock splits.

www.taguru.com

Taguru.com offers technical analysis from A to Z—an incredible free on-line course on technical analysis. Every topic imaginable with lots of detailed information on understanding chart patterns. It offers definitions of numerous technical indicators, a glossary of key technical indicators, and a short primer on Elliott Wave Analysis.

www.thestreet.com

There are two reasons we consider this an excellent site for the part-time trader. First, a writer, Gary Smith, is a day trader. Smith is not a momentum trader, but more of a day position trader, entering trades in the morning and exiting at the end of the day. This site would be excellent for those of you who develop that trading style. Second, the other writer is James Cramer, a controversial figure because of his demeanor when he appears on CNBC. However, as a professional hedge-fund manager, his daily commentary is great: no nonsense, just straight stuff in the real world of high-level institutional-type trading that affects us all as individual traders.

www.undergroundtrader.com

The UndergroundTrader is the location of perhaps the best Web site trading room. Jay Yu is the founder. Please see "Trading Room Web Sites" in Chapter 4 for a comprehensive write-up.

www.upside.com

This site offers an on-line magazine dealing with breaking news in technical companies. You can get a free subscription to UpsideDirect, giving daily commentaries on what will drive high-tech stocks, the upcoming day's newsmakers, technology events, and headlines. Excellent information to start off your day.

www.viwes.com

This site is a great place to determine short interest on Nasdaq stocks. What is the short interest on any particular stock? Which stocks have short positions that have been increasing recently? Which have been decreasing recently? Is the market getting more bullish or bearish? News. Message boards.

www.wallstreetcity.com

So you hear that the mining stocks are strong today. How do you find out which stocks are in that grouping? This Web site takes the pain out of finding that information. Large listing of industry groups. Clicking on any industry group brings up a listing of the stocks in that group. Very helpful if you play sectors showing strength or weakness. Important during times of sector rotation.

www.zdnet.com

ZDNet is an excellent Web site covering the high-tech stocks. Its excellent daily free e-mail service, The Day Ahead, gives a heads-up on the markets and stocks to watch on the day the e-mail is issued. Read this before each market opening to help prepare for the day. The Web site has a wealth of information with some particularly good free news services. In fact, to check out a wealth of free e-mail subscriptions, go to this address.

tax preparations

Anyone considering day trading needs to understand the tax implications before they do their first trade, period. The following Web sites can provide that kind of information:

SureStart **www.greencompany.com**

A nationally represented company, Green and Co. specializes in tax consultation for day traders. We have heard Robert Green of Green and Co. speak in the UndergroundTrader chat room and found him to be extremely informative. His site has some excellent resources for learning about tax issues specific to day traders. If you or your present tax accountant is not familiar with tax strategies for day traders, you may wish to visit this site or consult with Mr. Green.

www.tradersaccounting.com
TradersAccounting.com says of its site, "What We Do . . . tax reduction planning for traders, entity incorporation in all 50 states, trader status analysis for active traders, and accounting and tax preparations."

> *Alternatives*—Check with traders in your community for names of local accountants who are well schooled in preparing tax returns for day traders. Be sure to get several good references from individuals who have actually had their returns prepared by these accountants before using them.

chapter 8

launching your day-trading business

develop a business plan

Anyone who starts a business is faced with a risk of failure. The more preparation you do, the less risk you take, and the better your chance of success. You have researched, prepared, and been trained in the basics of day trading. You are taking calculated business risks. You are not gambling.

You are approaching part-time trading with as much effort and research as it would take to build any successful business. You have committed to doing whatever it takes to get your business on a solid foundation. You are willing to put in long hours and hard work. You understand that success doesn't come easily or quickly. You are willing to build your business with patience and time.

You have read all the material in this book, and are ready to get started. We suggest you develop a complete business plan for your day-trading business. Write down your objectives, and set goals with specific dates for accomplishing each goal. Put together a detailed financial plan that includes the source and amount of capital you will use to fund your day-trading account. Write down your business strategies, and put together a detailed plan for accomplishing each strategy. Your plan should include specifying the hardware, software, brokerage selection, and trading room choices that you have made for your business. Your plan should cover the educational program that you will follow. Be sure you list all books you will read and training courses you will take, then list a date next to each for a target completion time. Write a specific strategy for simulation trading. Be very detailed with the strategies you will use in simulation trading and the total time you will devote exclusively to doing simulation trading. Write a separate strategy for transitioning from simulation trading to trading live. List profit objectives, milestones, and your criteria for success.

summary

This book has focused on teaching you how to start a day-trading business on a part-time basis. It has explored the advantages of being a part-time trader, and elaborated on the various options traders have available if they choose to trade while keeping their day job. The trend toward extended trading hours was detailed and explanations given of how this trend will increase the options available to part-time traders.

You have been given a basic introduction to the major exchanges, to electronic communication networks, and to Level II data, and you have been shown how this data is important to day traders. You have been guided through setting up your educational program, choosing books, finding the best educational Web sites, and choosing the best day-trading training courses. You know how to evaluate and choose a trading room and how to evaluate trading software. You have followed our **SureStart** suggestions and have put together a business plan for starting your new business.

You are preparing for real trading by implementing a thorough program of simulation trading. By using a simulation trading system, you will assess your strategies and skills before you have real money on the line. By following the detailed instructions on simulation trading you will reduce the financial risk that you may encounter as a new trader.

The book has shown you why success at day trading is most closely related to success at capital preservation. You have developed and implemented a tight stop loss policy, and are committed to the discipline of following this policy consistently. You have developed a system for evaluating your personal trading strategies and for improving trading decisions. You have experienced the thought processes that traders encounter when they don't react properly and don't hold to their predetermined stop loss. By taking this trip into the consciousness of one particular trader, you are now better prepared to face these situations in your own trading.

You have recognized that a large part of your success or failure at trading will be dependent upon your own inner mind. You have been shown the role played by the subconscious in controlling trading success. You have seen how thoughts flow inside the mind of a trader, and how those thoughts can turn a good trader into a losing trader. Most importantly, you have been given guidance on turning that downward spiral around.

You know exactly how much money you will need to get started trading and you understand the costs of both start-up and ongoing trading. You have been given crucial information about funding a trading account, including an estimate of how much money is needed to trade well. You understand the psychological implications of having an account that is insufficiently funded, and you have detailed your plan for funding your trading account in your business plan.

You have developed a plan for hardware, software, and Internet connections that will adequately support your day-trading business. You understand the approximate cost for each of these choices and are aware of its capabilities and limitations.

congratulations

As you open the doors to your new business, you know that you have prepared adequately for the challenge. You understand that there is risk in any new business venture, but you feel confident that you have put strategies in place to minimize this business risk. You move forward, you access your progress routinely, and you adjust your plan to improve your performance. You have successfully begun your new business, Day Trading Part-Time. We congratulate you on a job well done!

appendix a

summary of SureStart suggestions

Listed below are all the **SureStart** suggestions we make in this book.

books

The Electronic Day Trader, Friedfertig and West
The Disciplined Trader, Douglas
Technical Analysis Explained, Pring
The Underground Level 2 Daytraders Handbook, Yu

broker, Level I quotes

CyBerBroker's CyBerX

broker, Level II quotes

CyBerBroker's CyBerTrader

computer and monitor

500 MHz Pentium III, 256 megs of RAM
21″ monitor

Internet connection

ISDN

on-line trading rooms

The UndergroundTrader, www.undergroundtrader.com
(Most suited for short-term momentum trading)

The Momentumtrader, www.mtrader.com
(Recommended for overnight holds)

The Momentum Trader's SwingTrade room, www.swingtrader.net
(Most suited for conservative calls, particularly consolidation-breakout trading)

simulation trading

CyBerTrader
(Both with previous day's data [free] and live data [with opened account])

software

CyBerTrader

tax preparations

Green and Co.

trading strategies

Short-term momentum trading
Consolidation-breakout trading

training courses

(We do not have enough first-hand experience with these to give a **SureStart** suggestion)

informational Web sites

www.bigeasyinvestor.com
www.cbs.marketwatch.com
www.clearstation.com
http://finance.yahoo.com
www.tradingmarkets.com
www.quote.com
www.daytrading-part-time.com (author's Web site)

appendix b

Securities and Exchange Commission advice

day trading: your dollars at risk

The following extract was taken from Securities and Exchange Commission Office of Investor Education and Assistance . . . "Day Trading Alert and Online Tips," September 16, 1999.

> Day traders rapidly buy and sell stocks throughout the day in the hope that their stocks will continue climbing or falling in value for the seconds to minutes they own the stock, allowing them to lock in quick profits. Day traders usually buy on borrowed money, hoping that they will reap higher profits through leverage, but running the risk of higher losses too.
>
> As SEC Chairman Levitt recently stated in his testimony before the U.S. Senate, "[Day trading] is neither illegal nor is it unethical. But it is highly risky." Most individual investors do not have the wealth, the time, or the temperament to make money and to sustain the devastating losses that day trading can bring.

Here are some of the facts that every investor should know about day trading:

Be Prepared to Suffer Severe Financial Losses
Day traders typically suffer severe financial losses in their first months of trading, and many never graduate to profit-making status. Given these outcomes, it's clear: day traders should only risk money they can afford to lose. They should never use money they will need for daily living expenses, retirement, take out a second mortgage, or use their student loan money for day trading.

Day Traders Do Not "Invest"
Day traders sit in front of computer screens and look for a stock that is either moving up or down in value. They want to ride the momentum of the stock and get out of the stock before it changes course. They do not know for certain how the stock will move, they are hoping that it will move in one direction, either up or down in value. True day traders do not own any stocks overnight because of the extreme risk that prices will change radically from one day to the next, leading to large losses.

Day Trading Is an Extremely Stressful and Expensive Full-Time Job
Day traders must watch the market continuously during the day at their computer terminals. It's extremely difficult and demands great concentration to watch dozens of ticker quotes and price fluctuations to spot market trends. Day traders also have high expenses, paying their firms large amounts in commissions, for training, and for computers. Any day trader should know up front how much they need to make to cover expenses and break even.

Day Traders Depend Heavily on Borrowing Money or Buying Stocks on Margin

Borrowing money to trade in stocks is always a risky business. Day trading strategies demand using the leverage of borrowed money to make profits. This is why many day traders lose all their money and may end up in debt as well. Day traders should understand how margin works, how much time they'll have to meet a margin call, and the potential for getting in over their heads.

Don't Believe Claims of Easy Profits
Don't believe advertising claims that promise quick and sure profits from day trading. Before you start trading with a firm, make sure you know how many clients have lost money and how many have made profits. If the firm does not know, or will not tell you, think twice about the risks you take in the face of ignorance.

Watch Out for "Hot Tips" and "Expert Advice" from Newsletters and Websites Catering to Day Traders
Some websites have sought to profit from day traders by offering them hot tips and stock picks for a fee. Once again, don't believe any claims that trumpet the easy profits of day trading. Check out these sources thoroughly and ask them if they have been paid to make their recommendations.

Remember That "Educational" Seminars, Classes, and Books about Day Trading May Not Be Objective
Find out whether a seminar speaker, an instructor teaching a class, or an author of a publication about day trading stands to profit if you start day trading.

Check Out Day-Trading Firms with Your State Securities Regulator
Like all broker-dealers, day trading firms must register with the SEC and the states in which they do business. Confirm registration by calling your state securities regulator and at

the same time ask if the firm has a record of problems with regulators or their customers. You can find the telephone number for your state securities regulator in the government section of your phone book or by calling the North American Securities Administrators Association at (202) 737-0900. NASAA also provides this information on its Web site at www.nasaa.org.

glossary

about our glossary

We have given brief definitions to words that you would most often hear day traders using, including slang. By giving you a quick reference to a word's meaning, you can decide if you wish to the check the index for further reference to a word/s or visit one of the Web sites that we have listed that have extensive and detailed glossaries.

AON (all or none) A trade order to buy or sell a stock in one order or not at all.

ask (also called the offer) Price at which a market maker or individual/ institution through an ECN (electronic communications network) will sell a stock.

ax Key market maker in a stock, sometimes known as the hammer in a stock.

basket trades Usually referred to as an institutional trade: large transactions made up of different stocks.

BB (bb) Bollinger bands, a technical indicator. Bollinger bands are bands (lines) that vary in distance from a moving average based on volatility. During volatile periods of price movement, the bands move further away from the moving average, and during market lulls, the bands move closer to the moving average. Explained in detail under "Short-Term Momentum Trading."

BRB (brb) Be right back.

bear market Period of time when prices are generally declining . . . bearish.

beta testing of software Highly experienced traders willing to trade on advanced software not yet fully tested and developed. Traders report back deficiencies and suggestions for improvement before release of software to the public. Not recommended for most traders.

bid Price at which a market maker in a stock or individual/institution through an ECN (electronic communications network) will buy a stock.

block trade Large transaction of a stock in one buy or sell of that stock.

bottom fishing Buying stocks whose prices have bottomed out.

breakout A point where the price of a stock moves out of a trading range where the price was relatively stable. Breakouts can be up or down.

BTW (btw) By the way.

bull market Period of time when prices are generally rising . . . bullish.

chasing a stock Trying to buy (usually a fast stock) a stock moving up in price by increasing your bid after the stock has already gone up several price levels. Usually a fool-hardy way of entering a trade.

chippies Traders using the ECN ARCA (Archipelago) and trading with small share size. Have reputation of panicking during reversals of short-term trends.

closing a trade The trade transaction that exits a trader's position.

CNBC plays Traders trading on news from CNBC television. Widely followed by day traders.

consolidation A pause in price trending of a stock, during which the price movement is relatively flat.

covering shorts To close out a short position. Buying back a stock that you had previously sold that was owned by your broker. That is, you had borrowed the stock from your broker to sell it.

crossed market Situation where market maker's or ECN's orders for buying and selling stocks is not in balance; that the highest bid is greater than the lowest offer or vice versa. Nasdaq prohibits intentional crossing of markets.

CYA (cya) See ya.

Cyber CyBerBroker or CyBerTrader software.

daily charts Chart periods, one bar or one candle, are equal to one day.

DCC (dcc) Direct communications. A private message window between two traders. Used extensively with mIRC (Internet Relay Chat). Visit

Web site for more detailed information to use this free software: www.mirc.com.

dead cat bounce A tiny bounce or "false" recovery after a major decline in a stock.

dead zone Trading hours of approximately 12:00 P.M. to 2:00 P.M. EST that has low volume trading and less liquidity. Market makers tend to be more competitive against day traders. A time for day traders to proceed with caution.

divergence (in charting) When two charting lines grow further apart or extend in different directions from a cross-over point or close to a cross-over point.

double bottom A reversal pattern in a stock. It is a decline twice to the same price level usually followed by bounces. Indicates support at this bottom.

double top A reversal pattern in a stock. It is a rise twice to the same price level usually followed by pullbacks. Indicates resistance at this top.

down off the bid Market maker lowering his bid from the high bid (known as inside bid) to a lower price level on bid. Usually a bearish signal.

down to the ask Market maker lowering his ask (offer) to the lowest ask (known as inside ask). Indicating a willingness to sell. Usually a bearish signal.

downtick The stock's inside bid is lowered by one level.

dumper Stock that has retreated significantly, usually due to bad news or missed earnings, followed by an over-reaction by sellers.

ECN Electronic communications network. Independent electronic trading systems, which allow market makers, institutional investors, and private individuals to trade Nasdaq stocks. ECNs also allow day traders to post a price better than the current ask or bid.

EOD End of day.

fading Buying a stock on a falling price or selling a stock on a rising price.

float The number of shares outstanding for a particular common stock.

Fibonacci numbers A sequence of numbers where the following number is equal to the sum of the two previous numbers: 1, 2, 3, 5, 8, 13, 21, etc.

fill A buy or sell order has been executed.

fill or kill A trade order is to be executed, immediately and in totality, or be canceled.

Five-Minute Rule If you purchase a stock using Nasdaq's Small Order Execution System (SOES), you cannot buy more of the same stock using the SOES for five minutes. You can, of course, sell your stock during these five minutes using the SOES. The same rule applies to the sell side: you cannot sell more of the same stock using the SOES for five minutes.

FWIW (fwiw) For what it is worth.

futures For day traders, reference is made frequently to the Standard & Poor's 500 futures (S&P futures) and the Nasdaq 100 futures (Nasdaq futures). Futures are agreements to buy or sell specific amounts of stocks listed in these future indices for an agreed upon price at a certain time in the future.

gap down Current day's opening price is lower than the previous day's closing price on a stock.

gap up Current day's opening price is higher than the previous day's closing price on a stock.

gapper A stock that opens at a price higher than the previous day's closing price.

gap and trap The price of a stock gaps at the open, buyers enter, market makers bring the stock down lower, trapping the buyers who bought at the higher gap price.

going long Buying a stock with the expectation that it will rise.

going short Completing a short sale (see short sale) on a stock with the expectation that it will fall in price.

GTC Good 'til canceled. A trade order that will remain active until it is canceled by the initiator. (Be cautious about forgetting these orders, you may get filled when you had wished that you canceled this order.) This is a great designation for stop orders.

grinding Similar to scalping where the trader is making many trades looking for small profits of a quarter to a half point.

heat Sudden buying in a particular stock.

higher low Established when a low of a stock's price or an index reaches a trough that is higher than the previous low trough.

hit the bid Selling a stock at the current inside bid.

IC (ic) I see.

IMO (imo) In my opinion.

IMHO (imho) In my humble opinion.

IPO Initial Public Offering of stock. The first time a stock is traded in a public market.

inside ask Same as inside offer. The best or lowest price at which a market maker or ECN will sell a stock.

inside bid The best or highest price at which a market maker or ECN will buy a stock.

IRC Internet Relay Chat. Software that allows connections to various private chat networks. Popular among traders is mIRC. (See DCC.)

inside day A day in which the total range of a stock's price is within the range of the previous day's price range.

ISLD Island, an electronic communications network (ECN). Second largest ECN, used mostly by day traders.

intraday Information pertaining to a stock during any given day such as price, volume, etc.

Level I Shows current or inside bid and ask.

Level II Shows current or inside bid and ask as well as all market makers and ECNs at different price levels on the bid and ask.

limit order An order to buy or sell at a fixed price or better.

liquidity The ability to exit a position, preferably in a quick manner.

listed stock Stock listed on NYSE or American Stock Exchange.

locked market When the inside bid and the inside ask are the same. Nasdaq prohibits intentional locking of markets.

long A trader's holding of shares from a buy order in anticipation of the price rising.

LOL (lol) Laughing out loud.

lower high Established when a high of a stock's price or an index reaches a peak that is lower than the previous high peak.

lower the offer Market maker lowering his offer or asking price, to lowest asking or inside ask.

MA (ma) Moving average.

MM (mm) Market maker.

MO (mo) Momentum.

MSH (msh) Market structure high. A series of three prices: a new high, followed by a higher high, then by a lower high.

MSL (msl) Market structure low. A series of three prices: a new low, followed by a lower low, then by a higher low.

margin account A trader's brokerage allows a trader to buy or sell more stock than if he used only the amount of money in his capital account. The trader is borrowing money from the broker, usually an amount equal to the trader's account.

margin call A demand by the trader's broker for the trader to put up more money as his stocks have declined in value to satisfy margin requirements set by Federal regulation on the amount of credit that may be advanced by brokers to the trader.

market maker A Nasdaq member who makes a market in a stock and is required by Nasdaq to be both buyer and seller in a stock they represent. They can also trade the same stock for their own brokerage accounts.

market order An order to buy or sell a stock at the current inside bid or ask. Often used to make sure an order is executed. The trader does not know at what price the execution will take place particularly in a fast moving volatile stock. The market order takes precedence over all other orders. Must be used cautiously by day traders because of the unknown price at which the execution will be filled.

market value of a stock The total number of shares outstanding times the current price per share.

mIRC One of the Internet Relay Chat software programs used by many day traders. Also see DCC.

momentum Is the rate of change at which a stock is rising or falling.

moving average Shows an average price over a specific period of time. The time periods can vary. The longer the period, the greater lag between the average and the current price.

market structure high A series of three prices: a new high, followed by a higher high, then by a lower high.

market structure low A series of three prices: a new low, followed by a lower low, then by a higher low.

Nasdaq National Association of Securities Dealers Automated Quotations. Usually just referred to as the Nasdaq Stock Market.

newbie Someone new to day trading.

new market Occurs when a trader, using an ECN, places a bid or offer between the spread, thus creating a new market for the stock.

nick A chat or trading room nickname.

noise Gyrations in the stock market which cloud the interpretation of stock's trend or pattern.

NYSE New York Stock Exchange.

odd lot Less than 100 shares or shares other than share size of 100 share increments.

offer Same as ask price. Refer to ask.

off the offer A market maker that is at the inside ask or offer raises his price and is no longer at the inside offer or ask.

open order A buy or sell order that has not been executed or canceled.

order An instruction to buy or sell stock and in what manner.

order flow Refers to orders referred to and handled by market makers or specialists. This gives them the insight of how a stock's price may trend short term.

oscillator A technical indicator that shows the vacillation of a stock within a trading range. Helps to identify overbought and oversold conditions.

overbought When a stock's price has had a sharp rise and there are few buyers left, the stock is considered overbought and the possibility exists for a sharp price drop.

oversold When a stock's price has had a sharp decline and there are few sellers left, the stock is considered oversold and the possibility exists for a sharp price rise.

pinging Determining at what speed you are connecting via the Internet or frame relay to another location, such as your broker's server.

point The equivalent of $1.00 in a stock's price.

preferencing Directing an order directly to a specific Market maker via Selectnet. The market maker is not obligated to fill the order. It is at their discretion whether to accept the order.

print Refers to the actual prices of executed transactions. Shows on the Time of Sale (TOS) portion of a Level II screen. Can include time and quantity of transaction as well.

program trading Trades generated from computer and sent directly to an exchange's or Nasdaq computers. Often a basket of stocks from institutional investors.

price/earnings ratio (P/E) The ratio of a stock's present price to its per-share earnings over the past year.

price resistance line (see resistance line)

price support line (see support lLine)

refreshing Refers to a market maker staying at the inside bid or ask and continuing to honor the previous price quoted and transacted.

relative strength of a stock The price strength of an individual stock compared with the other stocks.

retrenchment A reversal in a stock's upward price trend.

resistance line A price level at which a stock has difficulty in penetrating. Stocks will often fall back in price after reaching the resistance line. Once a resistance line has been broken it often then becomes a support level.

risk reducers Supplemental trading strategies to reduce your trading risk.

ROF (rof) Rolling on the floor.

round lot Shares in multiples of 100 shares.

round trip The completion of a buy/sell order or short/cover order of a single position.

RTM (rtm) Read the manual.

scalp trade Also known as a short-term momentum trade. A trade for a short duration usually for a small profit: one-quarter to one-half point.

short sale or shorting a stock Selling a stock not owned by the trader by borrowing the stock from the broker with the intent of replacing the stock at a lower price than it was borrowed. The profit to the trader is the difference in the shorting price and the price to which stock falls and the trader repurchases the stock. When the stock is repurchased it is called covering the short. Should the stock rise in price after shorting it, the trader will have a loss should he buy it back at a price higher than the shorting price. Shorting is possible only on an uptick.

short squeeze Occurs when holders of a short sale are faced with their stock's participating in a rapid rise. This causes many of these short holders to cover their losses, causing the price of the stock to go even higher. The remaining short holders are pressured (squeezed) as their losses increase until they too cover their short position.

short-term momentum trade A trade for a short duration, usually for several minutes for a small profit: $1/8$ to $1/2$ point.

sideways market Stock prices are relatively flat, with no definitive upward or downward trend.

SEC Securities and Exchange Commission.

sleeping with a stock A day trader holding a stock overnight.

SNET SelectNet. A trader can send buy or sell orders directly to market makers. Market makers are not obligated to fill the orders.

SOES Small order execution system. Applicable only with Nasdaq stocks. It is a mandatory system requiring a market maker to fill orders on the inside bid or ask on a first-come, first-served basis. The maximum number of shares that can be SOES'd is 1,000 shares. Some stocks cannot be SOES'd for 1,000 shares. The number of shares that can be SOES'd can be found in the Level II stock box, usually as a "T" number such as T2, meaning 200 shares is the maximum number of shares that can be SOES'd on that stock.

SPOOS (spoos) Standard & Poor's 500 futures index.

spread The difference between the inside bid and the inside ask.

stairstepping In an upward trending stock, a rise in price, then a leveling off and rising again. Charting of the stock's price pattern looks like stairs.

STICK (stick) One dollar per share.

Standard & Poor's 500 Index (S&P 500) An index of the 500 largest and most actively traded stocks on the NYSE.

Standard & Poor's 500 Futures Index Futures contracts that trade based on the underlying stock index of the S&P 500.

stochastics A technical indicator that compares the current price of a stock to its trading range over a given time period in the past. It is an oscillator that shows short-term momentum of a stock within a trading range.

stock splits An increase in a company's shares without any change in shareholder's equity.

STONE (stone) One thousand dollars.

stop The preset price at which you will exit the trade, based on keeping a specific maximum stop loss.

stop loss A predetermined amount that a trader is willing to lose in a trade should it go against him. The most important discipline a trader can keep.

support line A stock's price level that resists penetration as a stock falls in price. When broken it often ends up being a stock's price resistance level when the stock turns back up.

SureStart A concise recommendation for the best product or service offered in a particular category.

swing trade Holding a position overnight or for several days.

taking it home Holding a stock overnight.

teenie One $^1/_{16}$.

TIA (tia) Thanks in advance.

tick An incremental rise or fall in price movement of a stock.

tier limit The amount of stock that can be ordered via SOES from a market maker. Usually found in the stock box as a "T" number. Example: T2 means that you can SOES 200 shares of the stock. Using more than the tier limit of a stock can cause order cancellations.

thinly traded stock Not much activity in the stock, little liquidity in the stock.

Time of Sales Refers to the actual prices and time of executed transactions as they occur. They appear on the Level II screen.

TOS (tos) Time of Sales.

trailing stops A stop loss that follows the price of a stock as it moves up if going long, and a stop loss that follows the price of a stock as it moves down if a trader is short the stock. For example, setting a stop that executes a sell order whenever the bid drops one-quarter point from its highest level.

trending A stock's price is consistently going in one direction, either up or down.

trend line A line drawn between or close to important price points on a graph. Either high price points for an upward trending line or low price points for a downward trending line.

TRIN A measurement of advancing stocks divided by declining stocks with volume of each as a consideration. Also known as the ARMS index. (0.50 = heavy buying), (under 1.0 = buying), (1.0 = neutral), (over 1.0 = selling), (1.50 = heavy selling).

uptick The inside bid of a stock is raised one level.

up to bid Market maker is moving his current bid to the inside bid.

volatility A measurement of a stock's price fluctuation over a given period of time.

whipsaw Losing money on both sides of a trade due to a stock's volatility.

WTG (wtg) Way to go.

bibliography

Douglas, Mark. *The Disciplined Trader*. New York: New York Institute of Finance, Simon & Schuster, 1990.

Elder, A. *Trading for a Living*. New York: John Wiley & Sons, 1993.

Friedfertig, M. and G. West. *The Electronic Day Trader*. New York: McGraw-Hill, 1998.

Friedfertig, Marc and George West. *Electronic Day Trader's Secrets*. New York: McGraw-Hill, 1999.

Lefèvre, Edwin. *Reminiscences of a Stock Operator*. New York: John Wiley & Sons, 1994.

Nison, Steve. *Beyond Candlesticks*. New York: John Wiley & Sons, 1994.

———. *Japanese Candlestick Charting Techniques*. New York: New York Institute of Finance, Simon & Schuster, 1991.

Ping, M. *Introduction to Technical Analysis*. New York: McGraw-Hill, 1998.

Rudd, Barry. *Stock Patterns for Day Trading*. Greenville, SC: Traders Press, 1998.

Yu, Jea. *The Underground Level 2 Daytraders Handbook*. Wheaton, MD: PredatorCorp. 1998.

index